RUSTIC RETREATS

A BUILD-IT-YOURSELF GUIDE

STOREY
BOOKS

Schoolhouse Road
Pownal, Vermont 05261

*The mission of Storey Communications is to serve our customers
by publishing practical information that encourages personal
independence in harmony with the environment.*

Edited by Jake Chapline, Elizabeth McHale, and
    Janet Lape
Cover design by Rob Johnson Design
Cover photograph by David Hense
Text design by Mark Tomasi
Text production by Eugenie Delaney
Production assistance by Eileen Clawson, Deborah
    Daly, and Lara Gibson
Illustrations by David Stiles

The information in this book is true and complete to
the best of our knowledge. All recommendations are
made without guarantee on the part of the author or
Storey Books. The author and publisher disclaim any
liability in connection with the use of this information. For additional information please contact Storey
Books, Schoolhouse Road, Pownal, Vermont 05261.

Storey Books are available for special premium and
promotional uses and for customized editions. For
further information, please call Storey's Custom
Publishing Department at 1-800-793-9396.

Printed in the United States by Bawden Printing
10 9 8 7 6 5 4 3 2 1

Library of Congress Cataloging-in-Publication Data

Stiles, David R.
    Rustic retreats : a build-it-yourself guide / David and Jeanie
Stiles.
        p.   cm.
    ISBN 1-58017-035-8 (pbk. : alk. paper)
    1. Second homes — Design and construction — Amateurs'
manuals. 2. House construction — Amateurs' manuals. I. Stiles,
Jeanie. II. Title.
TH4835.S76 1998
690'.872—dc21   98-15720
                                                            CIP

Contents

To Lief Anne, our daughter,

full of creative ideas, always open for adventure,

and never at a loss for ways to design a creative shelter.

ACKNOWLEDGMENTS

Our thanks go to Elizabeth McHale,
for her encouragement, support, and wisdom
and to Jake Chapline
for his skillful insight and construction expertise.
Also to John Henry
for sharing his knowledge of log cabins
and to John Pellegrino
for his inspirational tipi stories.

Introduction

We have a secret place, a weekend retreat where we can escape from city life. Twenty-five years ago, we bought land shaded by dogwoods and maple trees, overlooking a large pond. We planned to build a house, but in the meantime we were anxious to use the land as a refuge from our hectic life in the city. We built a sauna hut on poles on the edge of the water. It is a simple design but contains all the essentials: a wood-burning stove, foldout bed and table, a chest to store blankets, and a front deck to take in our beautiful view. In the winter we cross-country ski or snowshoe through the woods to our hideaway, light a fire in the stove and in twenty minutes our one-room cabin is toasty warm. We spend the afternoon ice skating on the pond and come back to heat up hot chocolate over the fire. In the summer, we fish, swim, and canoe. Twenty-five years later, we're still doing the same thing. Who needs a house!

The appeal of a rustic retreat or hideaway is universal — Webster defines a retreat as a "withdrawal to a safe or private place." It is a refuge where you can meditate, dream, clear your mind of worry, and achieve a degree of tranquillity. Today, more than ever, we need to have a place to escape from our high-powered electronic civilization with its hectic pace. A rustic retreat can be a temporary escape from cell phones, fax machines, computers, and beepers.

The space we live in is an important expression of our life. Its truly essential requirements are few — shelter from the elements and protection from wild animals. A view of the sea or the sunrise or sunset is an extra. The rustic retreat you choose is your personal affair. We have included a range of designs — a simple platform in a tree can be built in thirty minutes, while the "writer's retreat" is a mini-home, insulated, heated, and more time-consuming to build. A temporary lean-to can be constructed in a few hours using an ax and materials found in the woods, while the Adirondack lean-to is a more permanent and elaborate shelter. Although these designs are all different, they have much in common. For instance, a tipi is much like a river raft. They are both made using wooden poles, ropes, and canvas. You wake up with the sun and go to sleep with the rustling of the wind on canvas. All of these rustic retreats, whether deep in the forest, in an open meadow, high on a mountain or on the water, surround you with the magic of nature and help you to escape from the pressures and tension of everyday life.

Generally speaking, the shelters in this book are inexpensive and can be made by one person over a relatively short period of time. It is not our intention to suggest structures that will outlive their builders, although in some cases, such as the railroad tie hut, that may indeed be the case. Most of these retreats are easily built and easily left behind when they have outlived their usefulness. The concept encourages innovation and experimentation in unconventional construction techniques, without risking thousands of dollars in the process.

The building of huts as presented here may be used by some as a springboard toward more permanent dwellings that might be built later. They offer a way to break into the highly technical and often mystifying field of residential building. On this subject there are many worthwhile books that you may want to acquire if your interests and abilities surpass the information presented here. The most outstanding books that come to mind are *The Owner Built Home* by Ken Kern and *A Pattern Language* by Christopher Alexander. Both of these publica-

tions deal with do-it-yourself types of housing alternatives to the average "builder" house available today.

As you read *Rustic Retreats,* you may notice that we have not always included specific dimensions or precise lists of materials in the various plans. This omission is intentional. Emphasis has been placed on clarity and simplicity both in illustrations and instructions, and the aim has been to help the reader to understand the basic design and to adapt it to various site conditions or limitations of building materials. It is quite possible that you'll want to combine the roof of one structure with the window treatment of another, or you may want to change a particular detail to suit your own preference.

We wish you years of pleasure in whatever kind of retreat you build.

About Using Pressure Treated Wood

Because of its rot-resistant qualities, pressure treated wood is a practical solution for supporting posts and framing that comes in contact with the ground. When using pressure treated wood, be aware that most PT wood contains CCA (chromated copper arsenate) and make sure to take all necessary precautions. These include wearing gloves and a mask when sawing through wood and washing all exposed areas of your skin before eating or drinking. It's also a good idea to seal the ends of pressure treated wood with a moisture repellent, to help lock in toxic chemicals and to prolong the life of the wood. Do sawing outdoors and cut wood over a plastic tarp so sawdust can be disposed of and does not leach into the ground. And, of course, never burn pressure treated wood.

CHAPTER 1

Some Essentials

I went to the woods because I wished to live deliberately,
to front only the essential facts of life,
and see if I could not learn what it had to teach,
and not, when I came to die, discover that I had not lived.

Henry David Thoreau, *Walden*

Starting out with the right tools and materials, a sturdy ladder, and a practical way to carry supplies to your building site will help make your building project go smoothly. It is equally important to start a building project with an open, optimistic attitude. Building your rustic retreat should be a pleasurable, positive experience.

Essential Tools

It is very impressive to hear stories of backwoodsmen who can build a cabin in the woods in three or four days using only an ax and a sharp penknife; however, most of us do not possess the skills necessary to accomplish such feats. We must rely on good tools that will make the job easier and faster for us, which brings up the question, "What tools will I need?" This can be an important decision if you have to carry the tools any distance into the woods, since a box of basic tools can weigh as much as twenty or thirty pounds, not to mention the building supplies themselves. Therefore, the type of hut you build may be determined by the types of tools available and the accessibility of your site. Each hut will require its own tools suited to the job at hand. The list of tools should be carefully considered beforehand, as it can be an exasperating experience to get halfway through a day's work and realize that you have overlooked a vital tool, making it impossible to continue.

Power Tools vs. Hand Tools

Since most of these huts are likely to be built in the woods, there will probably be no electricity available to run power tools. There are, however, many top-quality battery-operated tools available on the market today, all of which can be used at a remote building site, far away from an electrical outlet. Without electric power, the most difficult job you will have to do by hand will be boring holes. You can accomplish this either by pre-drilling pieces back home or by using a battery-operated power drill. Most power drills can be used continuously for two hours without recharging them, and by bringing along an extra battery pack, you can double the working time. Another solution is to buy or rent an electric generator that can be connected to your car.

The lack of electricity should not discourage you in the slightest if you have provided yourself with battery-operated tools or with good hand tools that you have kept in good condition.

Which Hand Tools?

The most important hand tool for you to have in your toolbox is a crosscut handsaw with which you can do most of your cutting. You can do yourself a great favor if you buy a top-quality crosscut saw with Teflon coating or a stainless steel blade and ten teeth per inch. A sharp saw can make all the difference in a job, and you will be cutting practically as fast as you would with a power saw and with far less noise pollution. The sound of a handsaw cutting is a satisfying thing to hear in the woods, as opposed to the nerve-racking shrill of an electric power saw. When sawing by hand, you will have time to think and appreciate what you are doing, and you are likely to make fewer mistakes. If you don't want to throw out your old saw and buy a new one, then have it sharpened and set by a professional at your local lumber or hardware store. If you are cutting unseasoned wood and the saw begins to bind, spray the blade with silicone sliding compound or rub it with soap, and it will saw easier.

For ripping — that is, cutting along the direction of the grain — you can save time and energy if you bring along a ripsaw, which looks similar to a crosscut but has bigger teeth and a different set to the teeth. If you don't think you will have much ripping to do and buying a ripsaw is not one of your priorities, then just use the crosscut saw, but make sure it is very sharp and hold the saw more vertically when making the cut.

If you are out in the woods and you accidentally dull your saw blade by cutting through a nail, you'll find a triangular file useful to sharpen the saw. Although you won't be able to do as good a job as the experts, you can do a fair job of sharpening a saw yourself if you examine the angle of the teeth carefully and try to duplicate them exactly. You can use the same file to sharpen most of your other tools if necessary.

There are many other types of saws, each having a particular job that it does best, and if carrying them to your site is no problem, then by all means

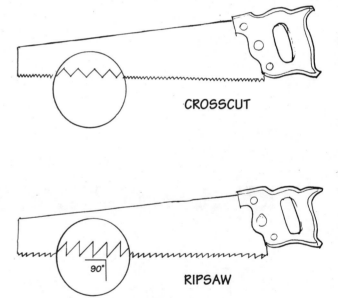

CROSSCUT

RIPSAW

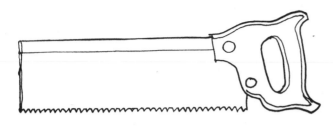

bring them all. The next handiest saw is the straight backsaw with fifteen teeth per inch (also called a dovetail saw). Although not absolutely essential, this is a great saw for making intricate joints, and the wood requires little if any sanding after the cut is made.

Larger Tools

Sometimes it is advisable to rent rather than buy a tool, especially the larger, more expensive ones. The advantage, besides the comparatively lower cost, is the fact that if the machine breaks while you are using it, it is the store's responsibility to replace or repair it, not yours. Also, you can rent a tool for one specific job, avoiding having to pay the full purchase price for something you may never use again. The disadvantages are, of course, the fact that you must know exactly when and for how long you will need the tool, and you'll have the bother of picking it up and returning it.

One of the best power tools you can buy or rent is a good chain saw, which can make all the rough cutting, especially trees, much easier. Don't buy a big one or you'll end up with a sore back very quickly.

If you feel that you cannot possibly build your structure without electricity, then you can buy a gasoline 110 V generator or rent one and haul it to

A list of hand tools, ranked according to their usefulness, might be as follows:

- Crosscut saw — 26″ long, made of stainless steel or coated with Teflon
- Hatchet-ax — 17″ long
- Hammer — straight claw, 16 oz. head
- Tape measure — 20′ long, ¾″ wide; and carpenter's pencil
- Swiss Army Knife — your choice of blades
- Army trenching shovel (folding)
- Combination square — 12″
- Level — with three vials — 36″ long
- Wrecking bar
- Block plane
- Chisel set — ¼″, ½″, ¾″, and 1″
- Wood rasp with handle — 12″

- Round rattail file
- Brace-and-bit set with seven auger bits
- Hand drill with eight bits
- Straight backsaw (dovetail saw)
- Screwdriver set — four piece
- Pliers
- Nail set
- Framing square — 24″
- Staple gun and staples
- Chalk and plumb line
- Snips
- Adjustable wrench
- Nail apron

your site. You must be the judge of whether the advantages are worth the cost and effort of transporting this heavy machine. If you're building in your backyard, you probably won't be faced with this problem. We built the Sauna Hut, described in chapter 4, using only hand tools and found it a most satisfying experience.

Ladders

Ladders come in three varieties: step ladders, straight ladders, and extension ladders. Although ladders are indispensable, some caution should be exercised when using them, since thousands of accidents occur on them every year.

Always test to make sure the feet of a ladder are resting on something level. Either dig a hole for the uphill leg or prop up the downhill leg.

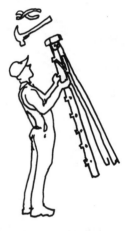

Never leave tools on the top shelf of a step ladder, since they can easily fall on your head when you are moving the ladder.

Never step on the last step of a ladder.

Fulcrum point

Never step on a ladder rung that is above the fulcrum point. The ladder will flip out at the bottom and slide off the roof on which it is leaning.

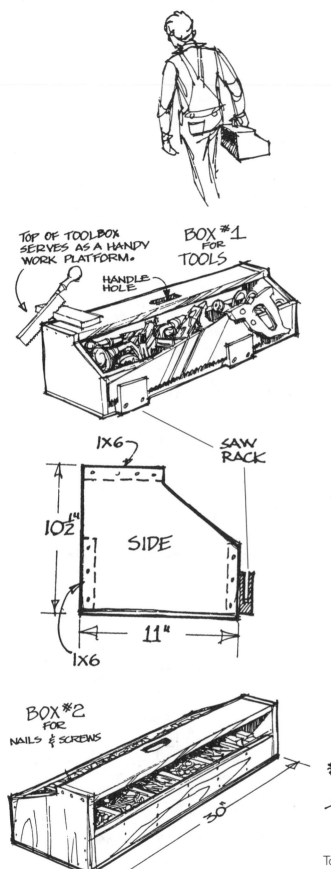

TOP OF TOOLBOX SERVES AS A HANDY WORK PLATFORM.

HANDLE HOLE

BOX #1 FOR TOOLS

1X6

SAW RACK

$10\frac{1}{2}"$

SIDE

11"

1X6

BOX #2 FOR NAILS & SCREWS

30"

Getting There

Once you have assembled your supply of tools, your next problem is how to get them, yourself, and your building materials to the building site you have chosen. In planning any construction out in the woods, this aspect is often overlooked, but it requires some thoughtful consideration. You may be faced with a two- or three-mile trek carrying as much as 300 pounds of building supplies and tools.

Where you build and what type of hut you decide to construct will dictate how you will handle this problem. Perhaps you can lash two canoes together to form a raft and float the materials to the site. Perhaps you just happen to know someone who owns an airplane and will airdrop them onto your site. If the terrain and access permit, you might make it through with a four-wheel-drive or all-terrain vehicle. If your site is in the snow country, maybe you can haul the materials by toboggan in the winter and build during the summer.

Toolbox

Even if your building site is only a hundred yards from the road, you will still need something to carry your tools. You could manage with an old box. However, if you have some boards around and an hour to spend, you might spare yourself some time and inconvenience later on by making two toolboxes like the ones shown here. They have several features that make them more practical than the average toolbox.

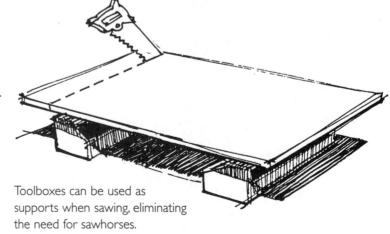

Toolboxes can be used as supports when sawing, eliminating the need for sawhorses.

Handcart

One means of transportation that you might want to consider is a handcart. It's tall enough to roll over rough terrain and can also be useful later when you are gathering firewood. This handcart can be made in one day and costs very little. It is capable of moving up to 500 pounds of material relatively easily, because the load is directly over the wheels. It can even be used to pry and lift up large rocks or to carry trees.

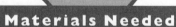

Materials Needed

Part	Quantity	Description
Interior frame	2	6' 2×4
Outriggers	2	40" 2×4
Spacer blocks	8	6" 2×4
Cross pieces	2	29" 2×4
Floor, sides, end panels		4'×8' sheet ¾" pressure treated plywood
Braces	4	17" 2×4
Cleats	8	¾"×¾"×14"
Handle	1	1½" diameter wood pole, 33" long
Wheels	2	Used 26" diameter bicycle wheels
Axle supports	4	5" galvanized corner brackets
Other materials		1¼" galvanized deck screws
		2½" galvanized deck screws
		Construction adhesive

Handcart Assembly

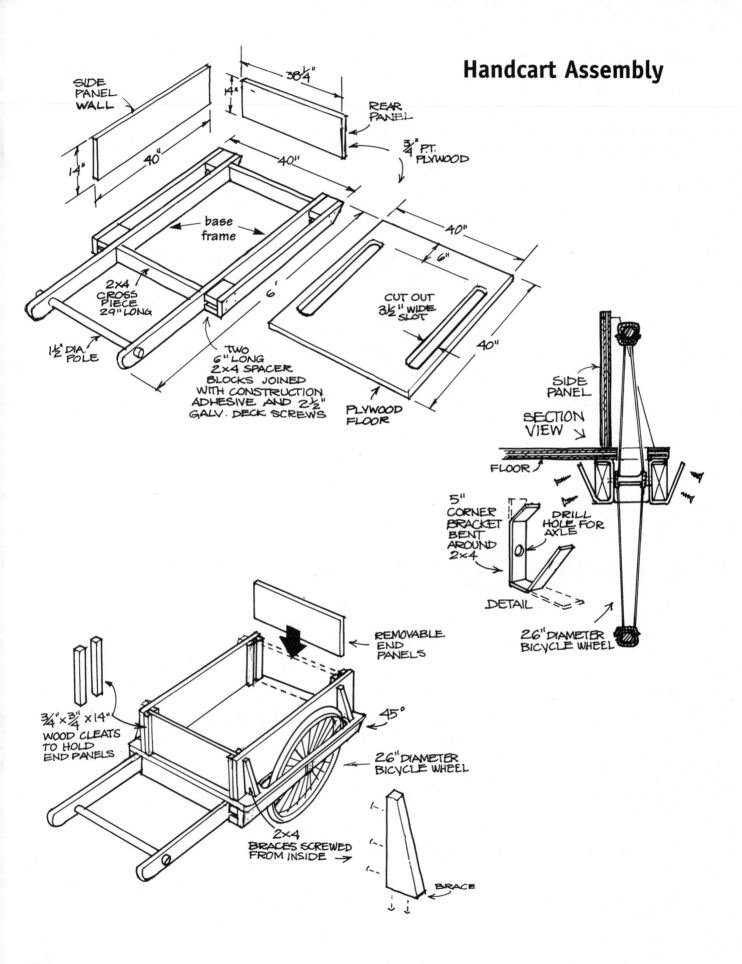

SIDE PANEL WALL

40"

14"

38¼"

4"

REAR PANEL

¾" P.T. PLYWOOD

40"

base frame

2×4 CROSS PIECE 29" LONG

1½" DIA. POLE

6'

40"

6"

CUT OUT 3½" WIDE SLOT

40"

PLYWOOD FLOOR

TWO 6" LONG 2×4 SPACER BLOCKS JOINED WITH CONSTRUCTION ADHESIVE AND 2½" GALV. DECK SCREWS

SIDE PANEL

SECTION VIEW

FLOOR

DRILL HOLE FOR AXLE

5" CORNER BRACKET BENT AROUND 2×4

DETAIL

26" DIAMETER BICYCLE WHEEL

REMOVABLE END PANELS

¾" × ¾" × 14" WOOD CLEATS TO HOLD END PANELS

45°

26" DIAMETER BICYCLE WHEEL

2×4 BRACES SCREWED FROM INSIDE

BRACE

1. Construct the base frame out of 2×4s. Secure with 2½″ galvanized deck screws and construction adhesive.

2. To support the ends of the bicycle wheel axles, attach each axle end to a simple homemade metal support. Use a hammer to bend a 5″ metal corner bracket around each 2×4. Bore a hole in each bracket, large enough to accept the end of the axle.

3. Cut the plywood for the floor, 40″×40″. With a jigsaw, cut a slot in the plywood for the wheel on each side and nail it to the base frame.

4. Make the walls of the cart by cutting two pieces of plywood, 14″×40″, and securing them to the floor with screws from underneath.

5. Form slots to hold the removable end panels by nailing wooden cleats to the sides of the cart at each corner.

6. Make braces for the side panels from scrap 2×4 and screw on from inside the cart.

Removable front and rear end panels allow long trees and lumber to be moved with ease.

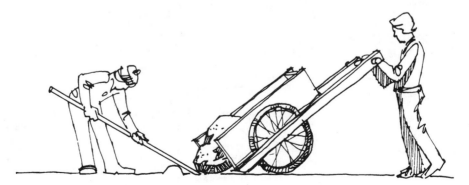

Heavy objects are no problem. They are pried up into the cart and balanced over the axle, making the cart easy to roll.

CHAPTER 2

Basic Building Techniques

Just like a perfect golf swing or a good tennis stroke, sawing a straight,
clean cut through a piece of lumber takes practice and concentration.

Joining Methods

Before joining two pieces of wood together, first think about the stress and the load that will bear upon the pieces when they are finally in place. For instance, don't nail a board into the end grain of another board and expect it to hold.

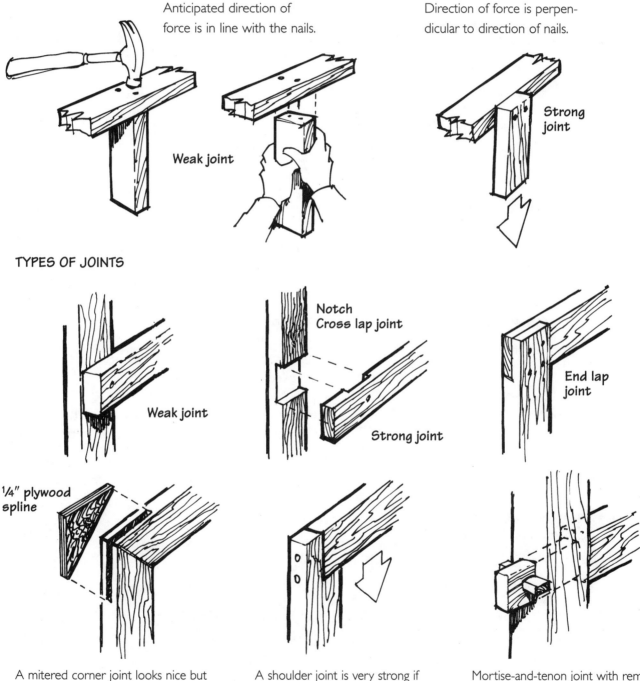

Anticipated direction of force is in line with the nails.

Direction of force is perpendicular to direction of nails.

Weak joint

Strong joint

TYPES OF JOINTS

Weak joint

Notch
Cross lap joint

Strong joint

End lap joint

¼" plywood spline

A mitered corner joint looks nice but is weak, unless a spline is mortised into the corner.

A shoulder joint is very strong if weight is pressing down on it.

Mortise-and-tenon joint with removable peg. This is difficult to make, but very strong.

Strengthening Joints

Joints can be strengthened by using triangles.

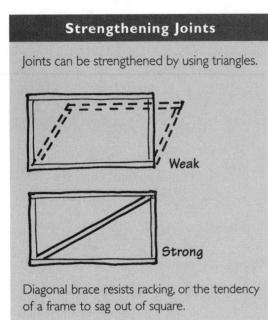

Weak

Strong

Diagonal brace resists racking, or the tendency of a frame to sag out of square.

Edge Joints

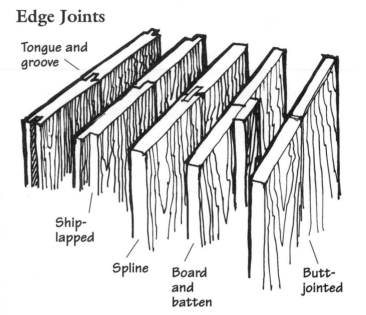

Tongue and groove

Ship-lapped

Spline

Board and batten

Butt-jointed

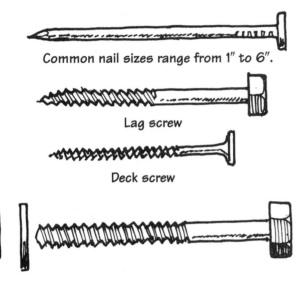

Common nail sizes range from 1" to 6".

Lag screw

Deck screw

Joints can be held together using a variety of fasteners.

Fasteners

Nails are quick and simple to use, but they must be used "in sheer," or perpendicular to the expected force. Use only galvanized nails and, if necessary, drill a pilot hole to avoid splitting the wood.

Screws have three times the holding power of nails. If possible, use screws instead of nails, not only because they are stronger, but also because they can be removed if you make a mistake.

Bolts are the best fastener to use, because they provide a permanent clamping force on the joint.

▶ TIP

If appearance is not a factor, use extra long nails and bend, or "clinch," them over where they protrude on the bottom side to give them more holding power.

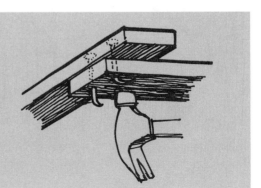

Windows

Windows are the eyes of a dwelling through which light enters and through which we see out. They should be carefully planned to be aesthetically pleasing from both the inside and the outside.

Types
Windows are expensive if bought at a lumberyard; however, you can buy used ones and install them yourself very inexpensively.

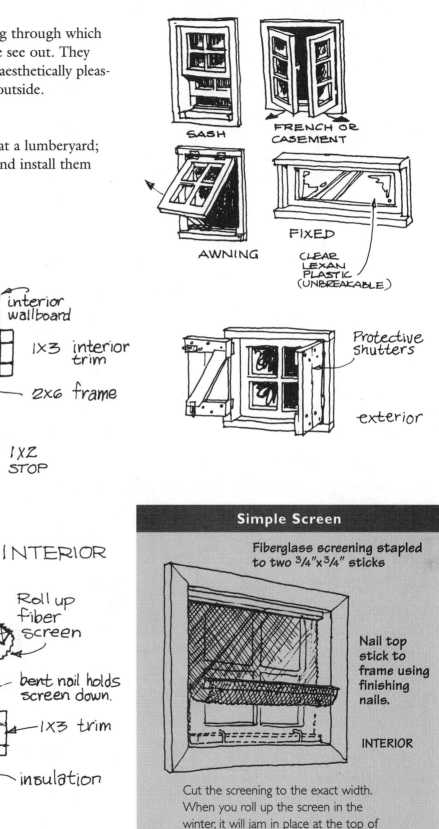

SASH

FRENCH OR CASEMENT

AWNING

FIXED

CLEAR LEXAN PLASTIC (UNBREAKABLE)

Protective shutters

exterior

exterior siding

30° bevel

sheet metal flashing

2X4

2X6

interior wallboard

1X3 interior trim

2x6 frame

Used window bought at scrap yard

1X2 STOP

INTERIOR

OPEN

EXTERIOR

Roll up fiber screen

bent nail holds screen down.

Drip ledge

2X6

2X4

1X3 trim

caulk

insulation

Side cutaway view of an awning window assembly

Simple Screen

Fiberglass screening stapled to two 3/4"x3/4" sticks

Nail top stick to frame using finishing nails.

INTERIOR

Cut the screening to the exact width. When you roll up the screen in the winter, it will jam in place at the top of the window.

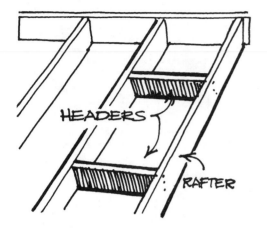

When framing the roof, add headers between the rafters to support the skylight.

Skylights

Many dwellings, such as log cabins, look cozy and bright on the outside but feel dark and gloomy on the inside because they lack windows. A good solution is to add a skylight. Even a small skylight can flood a hut with bright light and chase out the gloom. Skylights allow light to enter a room without sacrificing wall space and provide 30 percent more light than windows.

A very crude skylight can be made by leaving off a section of roofing material and substituting a piece of ¼″ Plexiglas in its place. Make sure the Plexiglas overlaps the hole on all sides by at least 2½″ and always caulk between the Plexiglas and the roofing material. A good product to use here, called glazier's tape, can be laid on top of the Plexiglas before applying the roofing material. It sticks well to Plexiglas and provides a continuous bead of caulk around the skylight. The top and sides of the skylight should be covered by whatever roofing material you use. The bottom of the Plexiglas should emerge from and lap over the roofing material.

Use aluminum flashing under the row of roofing above the skylight, or add another layer of roofing material.

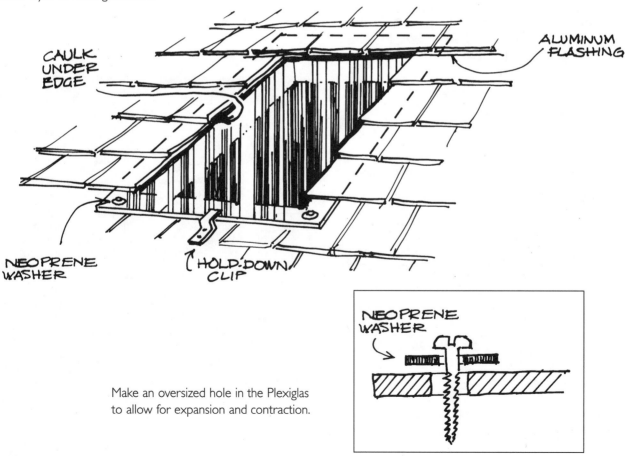

Make an oversized hole in the Plexiglas to allow for expansion and contraction.

Doors

A very solid door can be made by bolting 1×6 tongue-and-groove (T&G) boards onto both sides of a piece of ¾″ plywood, making the total thickness of the door a sturdy 2¼″.

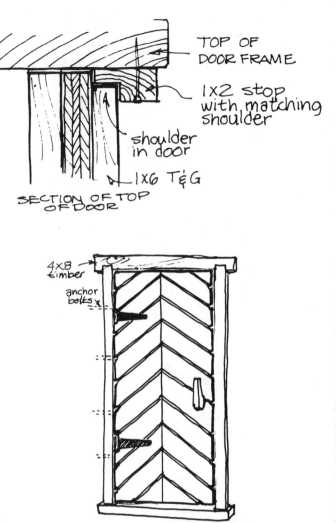

TOP OF DOOR FRAME

1×2 stop with matching shoulder

shoulder in door

1×6 T&G

SECTION OF TOP OF DOOR

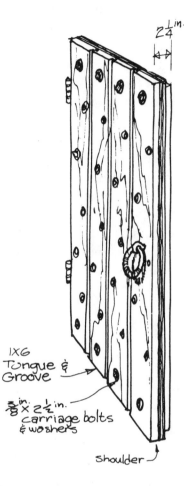

$2\frac{1}{4}$ in.

1×6 Tongue & Groove

$\frac{3}{8}$ in. × $2\frac{1}{2}$ in. carriage bolts & washers

shoulder

4×8 timber

anchor bolts

Doors with diagonal boards are harder to make, but they look nice!

TYPES OF DOORS

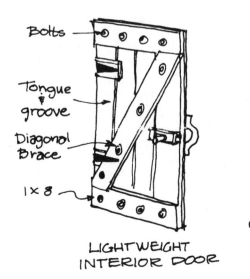

Bolts

Tongue & groove

Diagonal Brace

1×8

LIGHTWEIGHT INTERIOR DOOR

used brick

DUTCH DOOR

wire turn-buckle

SCREEN DOOR

Double Lap Joint

2 pcs. $\frac{1}{2}$″ × 3 with screen in between

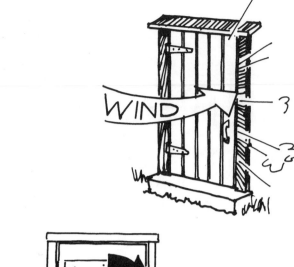

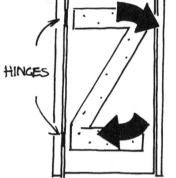

Hanging Doors

Be sure to mount the door so that it swings out. This way, when the wind blows, it will push the door against the hut and tighten the seal between the door and the door jamb.

To prevent a door from sagging, install a diagonal brace, which should start on the far side of the door from the top hinge and angle down to the bottom hinge. Since the door is always pulling away from the top hinge, use extra long screws at the top. The bottom hinge requires very little to keep it in place, since it is always pressing against the door frame.

An easy method for hanging doors is to screw the door hinge to the casing BEFORE you install the door. Then, prop the door in position and nail the jamb casing to the wall. Note: If you are using this method, make the door 1″ wider on all sides, so that when it is closed, it will rest against the wall of the hut. Add the remaining jamb casing and the top beveled trim to finish the door.

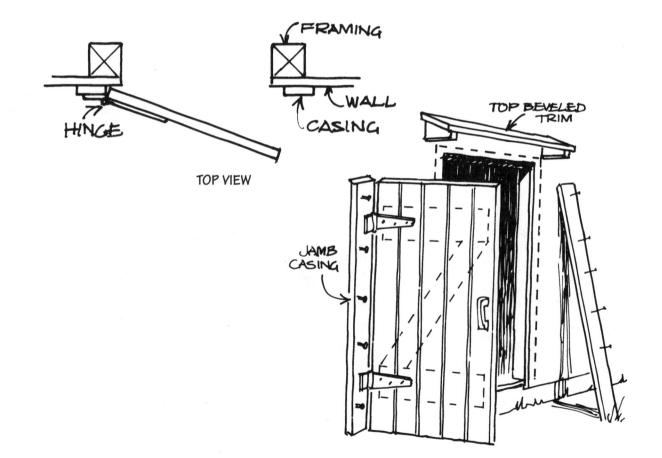

Roofs

Although it is easier to build a flat roof, it generally will not last as long as a slanted roof because it does not shed water. The object is to get the rain or snow off the roof as quickly as possible. Slanting the roof is the obvious answer. Even though it uses more material and can be difficult to walk on if repairs are necessary, a slanted roof is usually the best choice.

At a slight angle the water runs down the outside of the cup and back up!

At a steeper angle, the water runs free.

Water can run back uphill if the pitch is not steep enough and the drip edge is not long enough.

Rain water can rot wood quickly when left to collect, so be especially careful to use flashing (thin sheet metal) around chimneys, skylights, and valleys.

Bad   Good

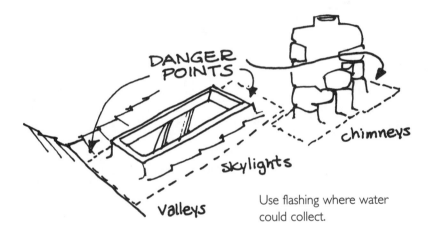

DANGER POINTS

chimneys

skylights

valleys

Use flashing where water could collect.

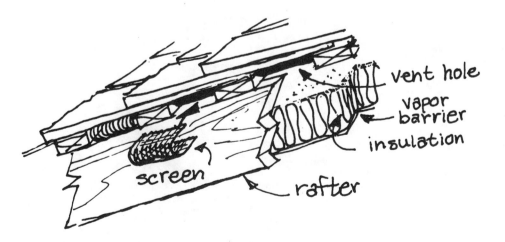

vent hole

vapor barrier

insulation

screen

rafter

Roofs should be ventilated above the insulation. Cover end vent holes with a screen to prevent squirrels and bees from getting in.

Wood Roofs

Since thin wood planks cut from a log tend to warp or "cup," this act of nature can be used to advantage to make board and batten roofs.

Long slabs of cedar bark can be peeled from dead *trees.*

SHINGLES & SHAKES

Cedar shingles

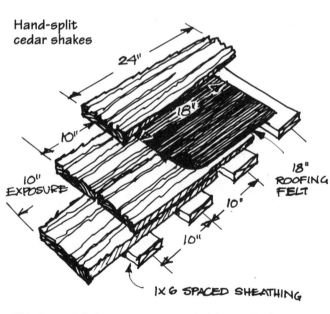

18"

1x4 SPACED SHEATHING

5½"

5½"

5½"

5½"

Birch bark is highly resistant to rot and was used by Indians to make wigwams. Note: Never strip bark from a live tree.

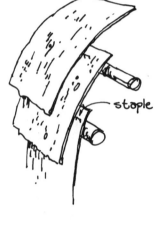

staple

Hand-split cedar shakes

24"

18"

10"

10" EXPOSURE

10"

10"

18" ROOFING FELT

1X6 SPACED SHEATHING

Shingles and shakes are recommended for roofs with a slope of 4"/12" or steeper.

> ▶ **TIP**

Use a 1x6 board as a straight edge to line up the butt edge of each shingle as you hammer it on. Nails should be placed 6½" above the shingle below so that the next course of shingles will just cover the nail heads. Make sure that each shingle overlaps the joint between the shingles below by at least 1½".

1"

1½"

Sod Roof

Sod roofs were traditionally built in parts of Scandinavia and were often found in early American frontier homes in Nebraska. Sod roofs, generally flat or with only a slight slope, have the advantage of being constructed from inexpensive materials and remaining cool in the summer and warm in the winter. Keep in mind, however, that a sod roof requires yearly maintenance and is more prone to leaks than a wooden roof. There is nothing more beautiful than wild flowers or Iris crowning a sod rooftop!

Six Layers:

1. Poles — 5″–8″ thick, laid as close together as possible.
2. Moss and dried grass — stuffed in the cracks.
3. Tar paper — each strip should overlap the previous one by 18″.
4. Heavy straw — laid perpendicular to direction of logs.
5. Mud or wet clay — packed down hard and smooth.
6. Sod — use 12″×18″ pieces, including any dirt that remains on them. Pack sod strips together as closely as possible.

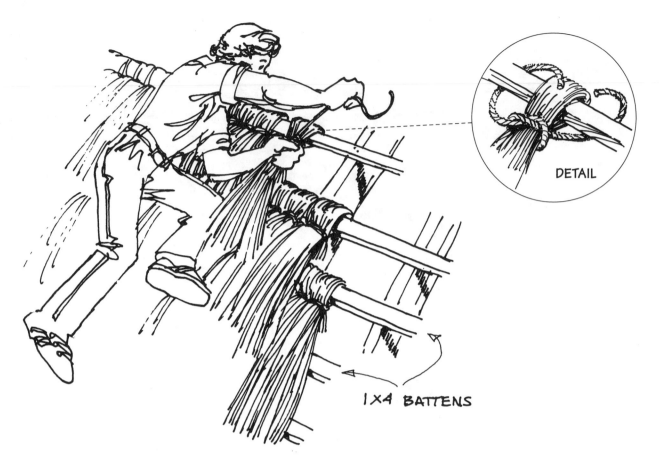

DETAIL

1×4 BATTENS

Thatched Roofs

Don't be afraid to build a thatched roof. Even though it is considered a lost art, it is still possible to do a good job with no previous experience. Thatched roofs were used extensively in the British Isles until a century ago, when they were replaced by tile and slate in order to qualify for fire insurance.

To make a thatched roof:

1. Gather a large quantity of straw. (Don't use hay since it rots easily). The straw should be 2 to 3 feet long.

2. Take a large handful of straw and make a loop with the ends by folding them over in your hand.

3. Bend this loop over a 1×4 batten.

4. Hold the pieces together at the "neck" and tie a half-hitch around the straw, using heavy string.

5. Continue the same process, bunching the sheaves together as closely as possible.

Each layer of straw sheaves should overlap the second batten below it. The top layer is bent over the ridge and tied securely to the underlying 1×4 batten.

Latches

If properly constructed, a latch like this will lock shut when the wind blows the door closed.

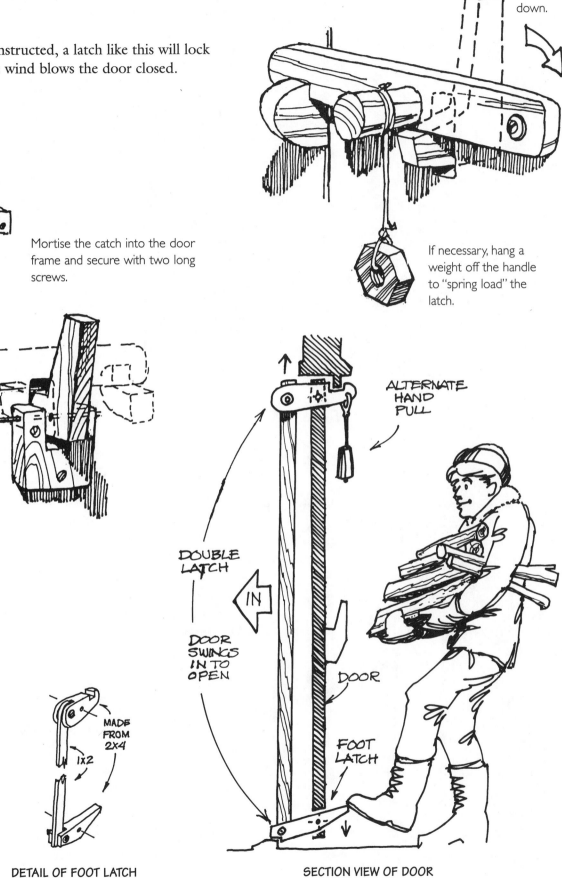

Pull handle down.

Mortise the catch into the door frame and secure with two long screws.

If necessary, hang a weight off the handle to "spring load" the latch.

PIVOT NAIL

ALTERNATE HAND PULL

DOUBLE LATCH

IN

DOOR SWINGS IN TO OPEN

DOOR

FOOT LATCH

MADE FROM 2X4

1x2

DETAIL OF FOOT LATCH

SECTION VIEW OF DOOR

Locks

A hand-crafted wooden lock can make your door unique.

SECRET LOCKS

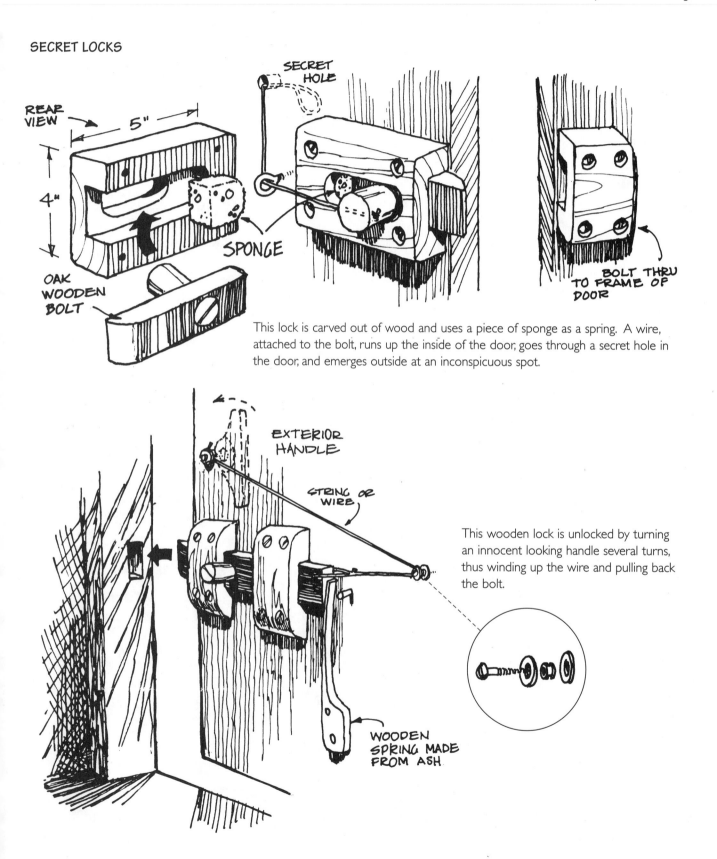

REAR VIEW

5"

4"

OAK WOODEN BOLT

SECRET HOLE

SPONGE

BOLT THRU TO FRAME OF DOOR

This lock is carved out of wood and uses a piece of sponge as a spring. A wire, attached to the bolt, runs up the inside of the door, goes through a secret hole in the door, and emerges outside at an inconspicuous spot.

EXTERIOR HANDLE

STRING OR WIRE

This wooden lock is unlocked by turning an innocent looking handle several turns, thus winding up the wire and pulling back the bolt.

WOODEN SPRING MADE FROM ASH

Combination Locks

These locks require turning knobs or sliding bolts in a special sequence to unlock the door.

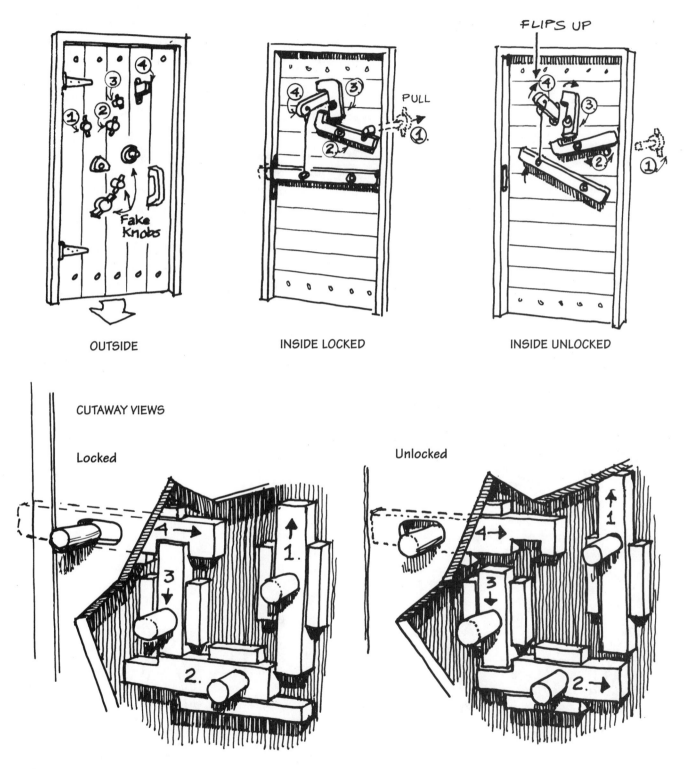

OUTSIDE

INSIDE LOCKED

INSIDE UNLOCKED

FLIPS UP

PULL

Fake Knobs

CUTAWAY VIEWS

Locked

Unlocked

The slide bolt lock is made while the door is being built and is covered by the front door panel so that only the four handles are visible.

Ropes and Knots

Many of the huts in this book require rope of some kind in their construction. Native Americans made rope by hand from the bark of bass wood, with a tensile strength exceeding that of manila rope. It is doubtful that the reader will go this far. For the more practical minded, here are a few tips.

For joining structural members that will receive constant wear, use synthetic ropes such as Nylon or Dacron, since they are strong and rot resistant. Nylon is best for making lashings to a tree, because it has some elasticity. One synthetic rope to avoid is polypropylene, which degrades in the sun, makes slippery knots, and in time produces tiny sharp "whiskers" that can cut your hands. Also, be careful about using manila rope. Although it is made of natural fibers, manila hemp has a tendency to rot from within, making the user unaware of its defects until a load is applied and it's too late!

FIVE BASIC KNOTS

Overhand knot
Sometimes used as a stop knot or to keep the end of a rope from unraveling

Square knot
Most popular knot — used for tying everything from packages to payloads

Slip knot
Constricts around the object it is tied to

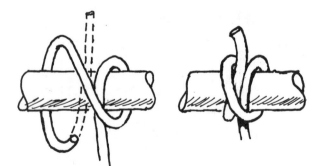

Clove hitch
Gets tighter as you pull on it, but comes apart easily when the pressure is released

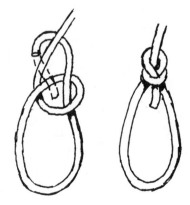

Bowline
A very secure seaman's knot used for slipping over pilings and posts

Lashing Together Two Poles

1. Start with a clove hitch.

2. Loop the rope over and under the poles twice.

3. Loop the rope under and over the poles twice.

4. Tighten the loops by wrapping the rope around the midsection several times, as shown in the illustration. Finish with a clove hitch.

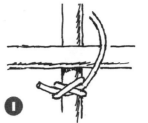
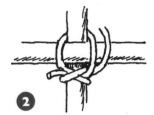
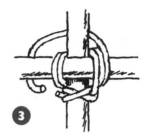
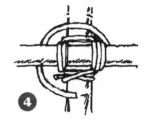

Whipping Rope Ends

Whatever type of rope you use, it is always a good practice to "whip" the ends so the rope doesn't unravel. With synthetic rope, this is a simple matter of melting the ends, using a match or propane torch. Use a flat putty knife to "paddle" the end of the rope while it is still melting, to keep the rope end flat.

Twisted rope, such as cotton or hemp, should be tied with wax-treated whipping twine, sold in nautical supply stores. Lay a long loop of twine alongside the rope and begin wrapping the twine around the end of the rope.

Wrap the twine tightly around the rope at least twelve times and slip the end of the twine through the loop.

Pull the other end of the twine, tightening the loop. Cut off the ends of the twine.

"Paddling" synthetic rope

Spool of whipping twine

"Whipping" twisted rope

Trees

Several shelters in this book require logs, which can be found in the woods and cost nothing, as long as you have permission to cut them. The difficulty is in finding *straight* trees that are dead but still standing and free of rot. In the summer, it is easy to tell if a tree is dead by the lack of leaves, but in the winter, it is more difficult. Try bending one of the twigs to see if it snaps, and make sure there are no buds at the ends of the branches.

Before cutting a tree down, stand back and observe it carefully from all sides. You can often tell which way a tree is likely to fall by observing that it leans one way or another, or most of the major branches are growing on one side. Make sure that the tree will not get hung up in another tree as it falls and that the wind is not blowing in the wrong direction. Before felling a tree, make sure all people, dogs, etc., are out of the way, and clear any branches from the area, to avoid tripping as the tree is falling. Never stand behind or in front of a falling tree. A few feet to one side is the safest position.

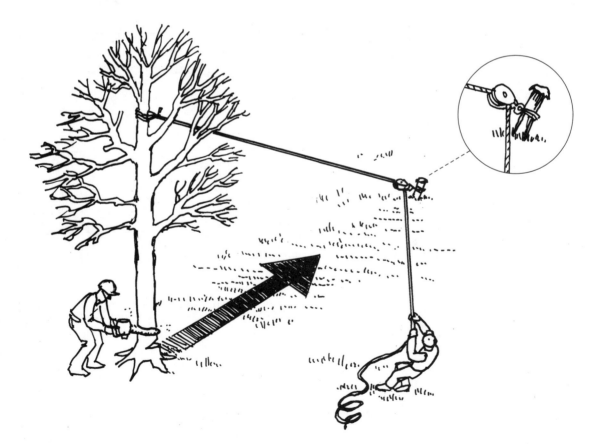

To help make the tree fall in the direction you want, tie a rope as high up in the tree as you can, and wrap the other end of the rope around another tree or a pulley. Have an assistant pull on the rope as you cut through the tree. Make sure your helper is standing in a safe spot, at a right angle to the tree's intended path.

To cut down a dead tree:

1. After clearing away any branches from around the tree base, make a 90° notch by making two 45° cuts on the side of the tree facing the direction you want it to fall. The notch should go no more than a third of the way through the diameter of the tree.

2. On the opposite side of the tree, make a cut approximately 2″ above the angle of the notch.

3. When you hear the tree crack or creak or feel it start to move, step away several feet to the side, never to the back or front.

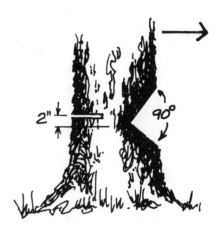

CHAPTER 3

Garden Retreats

We need the tonic of wildness. . . . We can never have enough of nature.

Henry David Thoreau

Garden Pavilion

An open, airy garden pavilion like this one can provide a person with many tranquil moments of com-
muning with nature and meditating, or it can be a
wonderful place for a secret rendezvous while watching the sun retire. It is simple construction, involving
only some cuts using a chain saw and a bit of bolting, screwing, and hammering. The roof is not
closed in, but instead is an open, decorative design
made of cedar beams, allowing the sun to filter
through.

Part	Quantity	Description
Corner posts	4	12" diameter locust logs, 8' long (11' long in areas where the ground freezes)
Roof beams	22 total	Peeled 8"-diameter cedar logs or 6x8 cedar timbers in the following lengths:
	2	12'
	2	11'
	2	10'
	2	9'
	2	8'
	2	7'
	2	6'
	2	5'
	2	4'
	2	3'
	2	16"

▶ *Windbreak (each panel)*

Part	Quantity	Description
Crosspieces	2	7' 2x4
Vertical supports	2	4' 2x4
Braces	4	1' 2x4
Screen	About 40	5' bamboo canes
Other materials	12–16 bags	Pre-mixed concrete
	8	½"x15" galvanized bolts
	8	½"x7" galvanized lag screwss
	32	8" spikes
	80	6" common nails

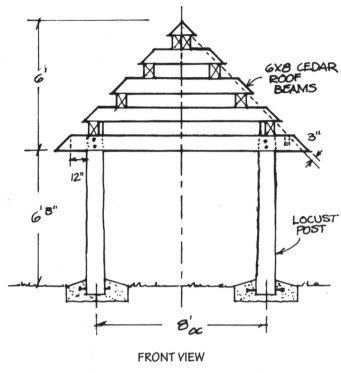

FRONT VIEW

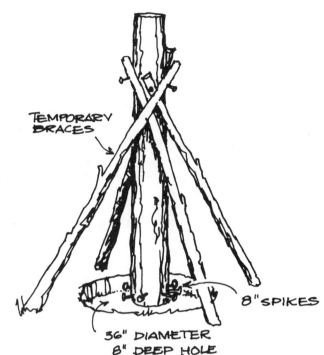

INSTALLING CORNER POSTS

Corner Posts

1. Clear a flat space and measure and mark an 8′×8′ area where the corner posts will go. Check for square by making sure the diagonal measurements are equal.

2. In frost-free areas, dig an 8″-deep, 36″-diameter hole for each post.

3. Prop the posts up, using temporary braces made out of sticks or scrap wood. Hammer 8″-long spikes, 3″ up from the bottom of the posts, to hold the posts in the concrete collar.

4. Mix and pour three or four bags of pre-mixed concrete into each hole, embedding each post into the concrete. Mound the concrete up toward the center, so rain will drain off. Allow the concrete to cure for several days, keeping it moist by sprinkling with water and covering with plastic sheeting.

Roof

1. Cut the roof beams to the correct lengths and mark the midpoint of each beam. Divide the beams into two sets. Lay one set on the ground with the midpoints aligned as shown.

2. Put a temporary nail on the upper edge of the shortest beam at the midpoint. Attach a chalk line to the nail and snap two lines from that point to the

Areas Subject to Frost

If you are building in an area subject to frost, dig a 20″ diameter hole, 3′–4′ deep, for each post and use a longer corner post. Instead of making a concrete collar, back-fill the holes with soil. Align the posts before back-filling.

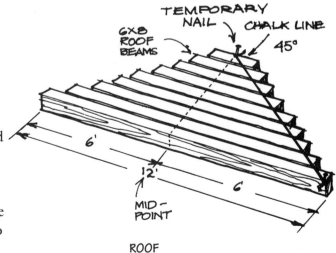

ROOF

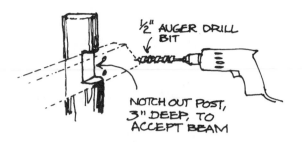

ATTACHING BEAM TO CORNER POST

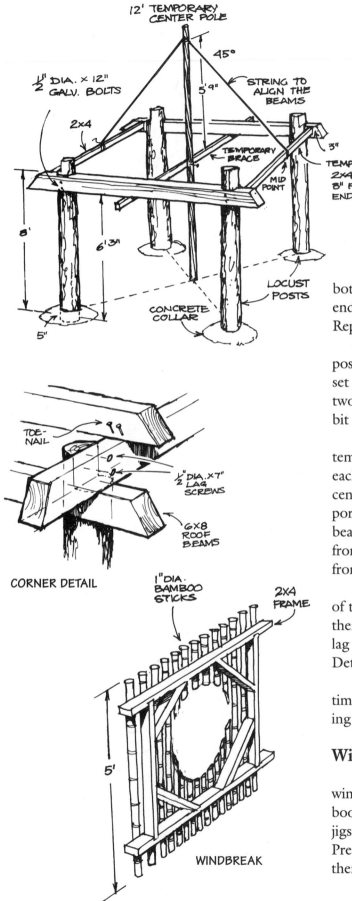

CORNER DETAIL

WINDBREAK

bottom corners of the longest beam. Cut off the ends of the beams along those lines at a 45° angle. Repeat this procedure with the second set of beams.

3. Make 3″-deep notches in the four corner posts, 6′3″ up from the ground, to accept the first set of beams. Attach the beams to the post, using two galvanized bolts at each end. Use a ½″ auger drill bit to pre-drill the holes for the bolts.

4. To align the remaining beams, attach two temporary 2×4s between the first two beams, 3″ from each end. Set up a temporary vertical pole in the center of the pavilion, holding it in place with a temporary brace nailed underneath the first pair of beams. Make a mark on the center pole, 5′9″ up from the top of the temporary brace. Run a string from this center point to the midsection of each 2×4.

5. Line up the previously marked center points of the next two beams with the strings, attaching them to the corner posts, using ½″-diameter, 7″-long lag screws recessed 1″ into the posts. (See Corner Detail.)

6. Continue stacking two parallel beams at a time. The remaining beams are attached by toenailing them to the tops of the beams using 6″ nails.

Windbreak

As an added feature, you can build a bamboo windbreak on one or more sides. Lay out the bamboo, measure and mark a circle, and use an electric jigsaw to cut out a window, in a size that suits you. Pre-drill holes in the bamboo canes, before nailing them to a 2×4 frame.

Grape Arbor
for Outdoor Dining

This traditional grape arbor provides a cool place in the summer to have a picnic or share a glass of wine with friends. It can be made using either cedar or locust posts and branches, stripped of their bark. Cedar wood can be identified by its scraggly, hairy bark, whereas locust has a rough, ropelike bark and is yellowish-green on the inside. Both types of wood are rot resistant and good choices to use outside where the wood is exposed to the elements.

Cedar posts can often be found at nursery outlets; however, if you are lucky, you may know someone who owns a grove or woodlot full of cedar trees that need thinning. Otherwise, avoid cutting down live trees; instead, clear the land of standing and fallen dead wood.

Plant grape vines, wisteria, or wild clematis, and train the vines to grow over the top of the shelter, providing a romantic spot to dine al fresco.

Part	Quantity	Description
Corner posts	4	10"-diameter (butt end) locust or cedar posts, 10' long
Braces	8	4" diameter, 3' long
▶ *Roof*		
Carrying beams	2	7" diameter, 12' long
Roof poles	6	5" diameter, 8' long
▶ *Railings (optional)*		
Poles	6	3" diameter, 10' long
Balusters	20 to 40	1½" diameter, 20" long
Other materials	12	8" spikes
	4	½"×12" galvanized lag screws
		Assorted nails
		Wood preservative
		Roofing tar

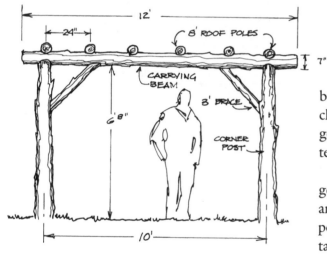

1. Begin by soaking each post's butt end in a bucket of preservative for 24 hours. In the meantime, clear a flat area and mark where the corner posts will go. The measurements for the arbor are 10' on center for the length and 7' on center for the width.

2. Dig four 36"-deep holes with a post hole digger, coat the bottom of each post with roofing tar, and set the posts in the holes. Temporarily brace the posts once they are plumb and backfill the holes, tamping down the soil as you add it.

3. Cut a saddle for the carrying beams in each post. Screw the carrying beams to the posts, using 12"-long, ½"-diameter lag screws.

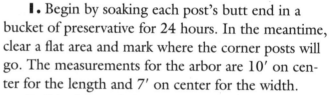

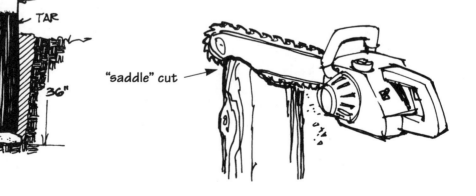

"saddle" cut

If the ground is too hard to allow you to dig a 36"-deep hole, cast a 24"-wide, 8"-thick concrete base in the ground and embed a 2"-diameter, 12"-long pipe in the center. Using an expansion bit, drill a 2¼"-diameter hole in the bottom of each post. Partially fill the hole with construction adhesive and set it onto the pipe. Use 7' posts if the ends are not going to be buried.

If any of the posts rest on bedrock, drill four ½"-diameter holes in the rock, using a masonry drill. Partially fill the holes with cement before inserting ½"x6" bolts. Allow the top 2" of each bolt to extend above the rock. Proceed as described above, casting the concrete over the rock and bolt heads.

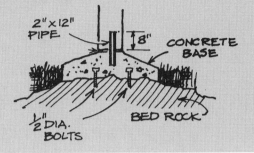

4. Use 8" spikes to attach the roof poles to the carrying beams.

5. Strengthen the corners by notching out the posts and beams and nailing 3' diagonal braces to them.

6. Assemble the optional railings. The number of balusters you need will depend on the spacing you prefer. Attach the railings to the corner posts by notching the ends of the railing poles and nailing through the notches into the posts.

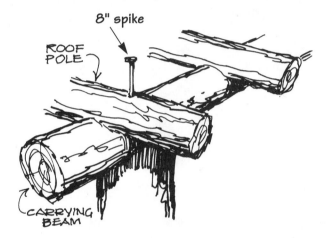

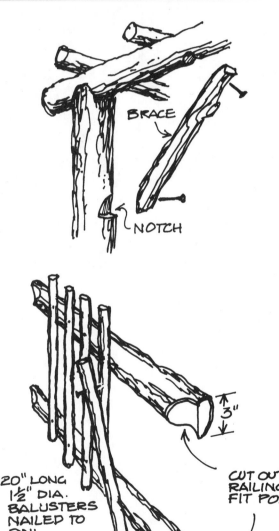

RAILINGS

Garden
Cordwood Hut

Originally designed as a shed for potting plants and storing garden tools, this hut is big enough to be used as an artist's studio or a writer's retreat. It is made of natural materials — logs for the sides and thatch for the roof. Begin by finding or buying four pairs of secondhand windows and plan the structure around them. Use two windows on each side to provide plenty of light. The timbers for the structure shown here were made by squaring off round logs; however, a lot of time can be saved by using 6×6 pressure-treated timbers. In either case, the walls are filled in with log ends embedded in a cement mixture. The roof is thatched, using the method explained on page 20.

Part	Quantity	Description
▶ *Foundation*		
Ground cover	1	6 mil plastic sheet, 10'×12'
Sills	2	8' pressure-treated 6x6
	2	10' pressure-treated 6x6
▶ *Floor*		
Crushed stone	1½ cu. yds.	
Cement	Two 80 lb. bags	
Sand	5¼ cu. ft.	
Bricks	About 360	
▶ *Framing*		
Plate beams	2	8' pressure-treated 6x6
	2	10' pressure-treated 6x6
Corner posts	4	6' long, 6x6 rough-cut fir
Other posts	4	6'4" long, 6x6 rough-cut fir
Horizontal timbers	7	4x6 cut to fit
Window frames		2x6 cut to fit
▶ *Walls*		
Logs	As needed	Mixed diameter logs cut 6" long
Mortar	As needed	
▶ *Roof*		
Rafters	12	13' 4x6
Ridge pole	1	10' 2x4
Braces	4	4x6 cut to fit
Spaced sheathing	44	10' 1x4
Other materials		Chicken wire
		Windows with hardware
		Door with hardware
		1x2 stops for windows and door
		1¼"-diameter hardwood
		Dowels for pegs
		Assorted nails

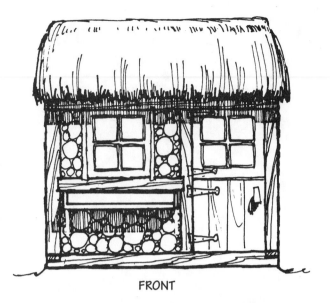

FRONT

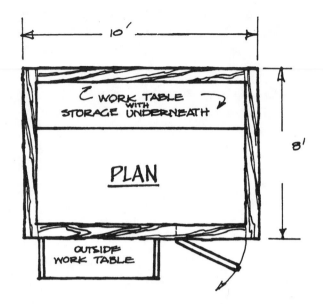

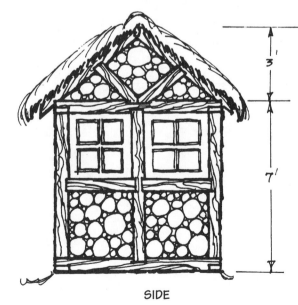

REAR

SIDE

Try to find windows that are roughly 3′×3′. Use one for the top of the front door. Cut and hinge the door in 4 places, making it into a Dutch door.

Foundation

1. Clear the ground of all debris and create a 3″–4″ raised, flat area the same dimensions as the foundation. Cover the ground with a heavy plastic sheet to protect the hut from moisture and insects.

PLASTIC SHEET

2. Build your foundation using locust logs or heavy, pressure-treated timbers. Make sure that the timbers lay on solid, level ground. Check that the corners are square by measuring the diagonals, which should be equal lengths.

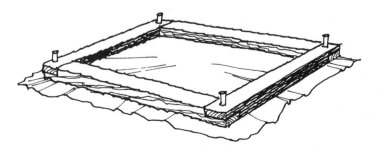

3. Use lap joints at the corners and join the timbers by drilling a 1¼″ -diameter hole through the center of the corner joint and pounding in a peg. The peg should stick up above the sill about 2″. When you begin framing, the corner posts will fit securely on these pegs.

Brick Floor

1. Fill the foundation with crushed stone to within 4″ from the top of the sills. Level the stone base and cover it with a layer of chicken wire.

2. Mix a batch of concrete using the proportion of one bag of cement to 2¼ cubic feet of sand to 3 cubic feet of crushed stone. Add water, keeping the mixture "stiff." Spread this mixture over the crushed stone, leveling it and making it approximately 1″ thick.

3. Allow the concrete to cure for one week, keeping it moist by sprinkling it with water and covering it with a plastic sheet.

4. When the concrete base is dry, mix a batch of mortar (1 part cement to 3 parts sand) and lay bricks in "two by two" pattern. Moisten the bricks before using. If you prefer, you can lay the bricks "dry" (without mortar), placing them very close together. Brush in a slightly moist cement/sand mixture, sweeping the sand into any spaces between the bricks and finally sprinkling the bricks with water.

4X6 RAFTERS

6X6 POST

OPENINGS ARE SAME SIZE AS WINDOWS.

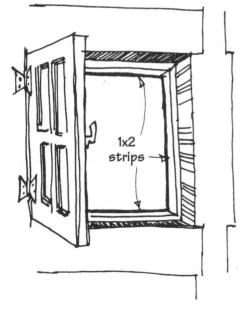

Notches for window-sill timbers can be easily cut using a chain saw.

1x2 strips

WINDOW

Framing

1. Cut all of the posts and drill holes in the ends for pegs. Note that the door post and the center posts for the rear and side walls are 4″ longer than the corner posts, because they will be notched into the sills and plate beams.

2. Cut 2″-deep notches in the posts to support the ends of the horizontal timbers that serve as window sills. (The position of these timbers will depend to some extent on your windows and door.)

3. Cut 2″-deep notches in the sills and plate beams for the door post and center posts. Drill a 1¼″-diameter hole in each notch. The holes in the sills should be 4″ deep, while the holes in the plate beams should go all of the way through. Insert a 6″ peg in each hole in the sills.

4. Set the posts onto the pegs in the sills, holding them in place with temporary braces.

5. Cut the plate beams to fit together with lap joints at the corners like the foundation timbers. Drill 1¼″-diameter holes through the center of the lap joints for pegs.

6. Set the plate beams in place and drive pegs through the holes into the tops of posts.

Walls and Windows

1. Frame the front and rear window openings with 2×6 lumber.

2. Frame the inside of the window and door openings with 1×2 strips to form stops and weather seals.

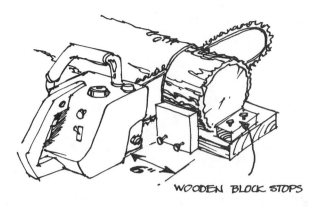

WOODEN BLOCK STOPS

3. Cut a number of 6″ long logs of varying diameter to fill the spaces between the framing.

4. Mortar the logs into the wall openings. Use mortar mixed in the same proportions as the mortar used for the brick floor.

Roof

1. Notch the rafters to rest on the plate beams and against the ridge pole. Notch the end rafters for the roof braces and drill a hole through each of the brace notches. Then assemble the rafters and ridge pole, toe-nailing the rafters in place.

2. Cut roof braces to fit, drill holes in the upper ends, and put the braces in place. Drive pegs through the holes in the rafters and into the holes in the braces.

3. Nail the spaced sheathing on top of the rafters.

4. Thatch the roof, following the instructions on page 20.

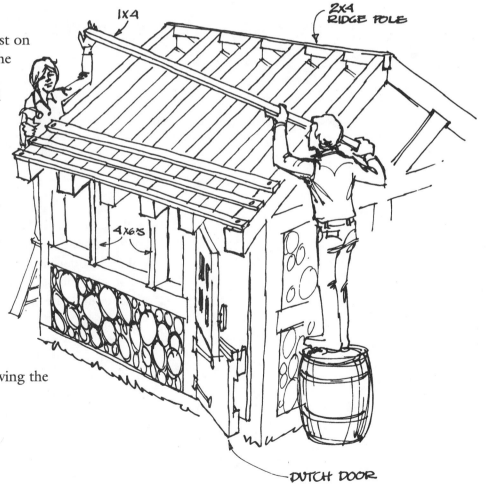

1X4

2X4 RIDGE POLE

4X6'S

DUTCH DOOR

Garden Bower

This light-filled shelter provides a comfortable place to rest while strolling through your garden. Although constructed with heavy timbers, it is simple to build. The thick rafters contrast with the delicacy of the latticework that frames the openings of the shelter. Two overlapping, translucent acrylic sheets, installed under the rafters, keep the interior dry. Seating can be built with flip-up seats and storage benches underneath, big enough to store some comfortable cushions.

Foundation

1. To form the foundation for the sill beams, dig two parallel trenches 7′ long, 12″ deep, and 10′ apart, and fill them with crushed stone.

2. Connect the two trenches with plastic drain pipe and run it to daylight.

Materials Needed

Part	Quantity	Description
▶ Foundation		
Crushed stone	About 2 cu. yds.	
Plastic pipe	Varies with site	2″-diameter PVC
▶ Framing		
Sill beams	2	68″ pressure-treated 6x6
Corner posts	4	45″ 6x8
Plate beams	2	8′ 6x8
▶ Roof		
Rafters	10	9′ 4x6
Roofing	2	4′x8′ sheets of ³⁄₁₆″ acrylic plastic
▶ Lattice		
Arch piece 1	2	³⁄₈″ clear cedar; 3″ wide and 10′ long
Arch piece 2	2	³⁄₈″ clear cedar; 2″ wide and 10′ long
Lattice	2	4′x8′ sheets
Lateral supports	4	Made like the arches from two pieces of ³⁄₈″ cedar glued together. Cut to fit (approx. 1′ long).
Vertical supports	2	2x2 cut to fit (approx. 2′ long)
Lattice nailers	4	1x2 cut to fit (approx. 7′ long)
▶ Side railings		
Rails	4	2x4 clear cedar; 52″ long
Balusters	16	2x2 cedar; 21″ long
Support strips	4	¾″x¾″, 52″ long
▶ Back railing		
Rails	2	2x4 clear cedar; 9′6″ long
Balusters	19	2x2 cedar; 21″ long
Support strips	2	¾″x¾″, 52″ long
Other materials	8	⅝″x7″ bolts
	4	⅝″x8″ lag screws
	10	½″x4″ bolts
		2″ round-head wood screws with washers
		Wood preservative
		Assorted nails
		Glue

Framing

1. Soak the bottom of the corner posts in wood preservative before installing.

2. Notch out each end of the sill beams to accept the corner posts.

3. Attach the corner posts to the sill beams using ⅝"-diameter × 8" lag screws.

4. Notch out the top of the posts and the top plate beam as shown and bolt them together.

5. To give the structure a traditional look, hide the bolt ends by recessing them 1½" in the wood and covering them with tapered wood plugs.

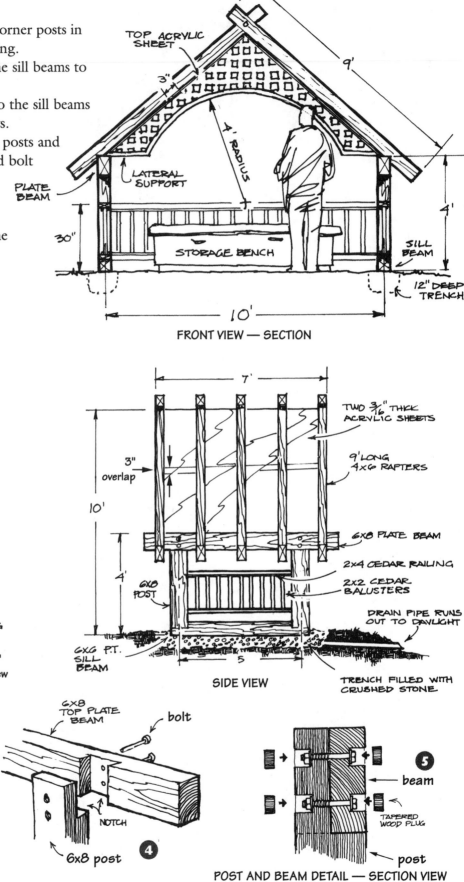

TOP ACRYLIC SHEET

3"

9'

4' RADIUS

LATERAL SUPPORT

PLATE BEAM

4'

SILL BEAM

30"

STORAGE BENCH

12" DEEP TRENCH

10'

FRONT VIEW — SECTION

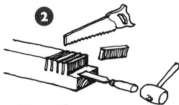

2

NOTCHING

6X8 CORNER POST

3"

8"

6X6 P.T. SILL BEAM

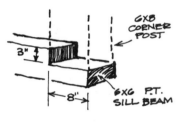

CORNER POST

WOOD PLUG

5/8"x8" lag screw

SILL BEAM

3

7'

TWO 3/16" THICK ACRYLIC SHEETS

3" overlap

9' LONG 4x6 RAFTERS

10'

4'

6X8 PLATE BEAM

2x4 CEDAR RAILING

2x2 CEDAR BALUSTERS

6X8 POST

DRAIN PIPE RUNS OUT TO DAYLIGHT

6X6 P.T. SILL BEAM

5'

TRENCH FILLED WITH CRUSHED STONE

SIDE VIEW

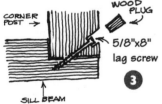

6X8 TOP PLATE BEAM

bolt

NOTCH

6x8 post

4

beam

TAPERED WOOD PLUG

5

post

POST AND BEAM DETAIL — SECTION VIEW

Roof

1. Cut a bird's mouth notch in each rafter to fit over the top of the plate beam. Toenail the rafters to the beam.

2. To keep the area dry, screw two pieces of ³⁄₁₆″ acrylic plastic underneath the rafters. The top sheet should overlap the lower sheet by 3″. Pre-drill the plastic sheets for the screws. (See Side View.)

3. Join the rafters at the top by notching and bolting them together.

Lattice and Railing

1. To make the arches that hold the lattice at each end of the bower, cut the four arch pieces, soak them in water overnight and then bend them into 4′ radius arcs. Glue each 2″ wide piece to a 3″-wide piece so they are flush on one edge, leaving a 1″ shoulder along the other edge. Clamp the glued pieces together for 24 hours.

2. Put the lattice frames together. The frame for each lattice includes a vertical support, two lattice nailers attached to the underside of the end roof beams, two lateral supports, and an arch.

3. Cut, fit, and nail lattice sheets to the front of the lattice nailers and the shoulders of the lateral supports and the arch.

4. Make the railings for the back and sides of the bower by nailing support strips along the rails with the balusters between the strips. Then attach the finished railings to the corner posts.

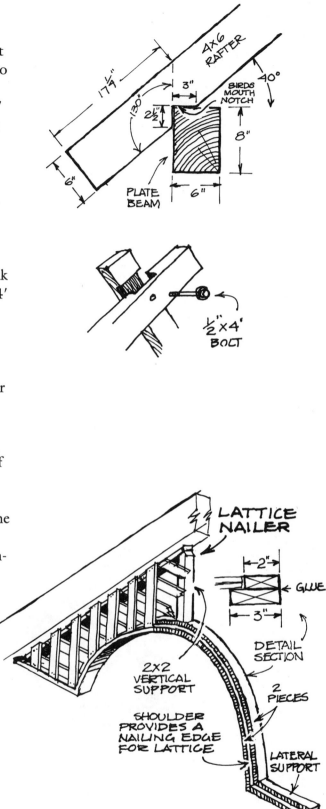

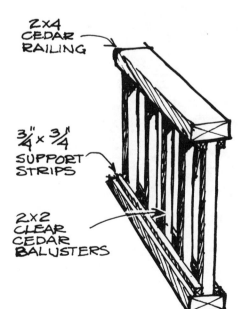

CHAPTER 4

On the Ground

Now I see the secret of making the best persons —
It is to grow in the open air and to eat and sleep with the earth.

Walt Whitman

Basic Lean-To

The basic lean-to can last one night or several seasons, depending on how well it is made. It is fairly easy to construct and can be made without chopping down any live trees. A very crude lean-to can be built in less than an hour using only an axe. However, one that will last more than one season and repel rain may take two or three days.

You can set up one lean-to across from another to share the warmth of a mutual campfire.

Materials Needed

- Two straight trees 6'–8' apart
- Two forked side poles 8'–9' long
- One ridge pole about 10' long
- Three rafter poles 8'–9' long
- Two side posts about 4' long
- About 25 crosspieces 1" in diameter and 5' long
- Hemp string, light (¼") rope, or baling wire for lashing
- Evergreen boughs for thatching

Construction

1. Use the two forked side poles to prop up the ridge pole between two straight trees, about 6′–8′ apart. Lash the three poles together.

RIDGE POLE

5 to 6 Ft.

6 to 8 Ft.

FORKED SIDE POLE 8 to 9 Ft. LONG

2. Lay three more rafter poles against the ridge pole, allowing any small branches to protrude upward to support the smaller crosspieces used in the next step.

Leave branch stubs on top, but cut off the ones pointing down.

3 CROSSPIECES

vertical post

3. Using a small hand saw or brush cutters, cut crosspieces and weave them between the rafter poles.

4. Add a vertical post on each side of the lean-to and bend in crosspieces.

5. Thatch the roof with evergreen boughs, starting at the bottom and overlapping them all the way up.

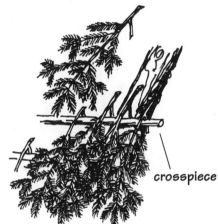

crosspiece

You can add to your lean-to by making a half-roof and sides.

On cold nights make a "back log" fire, using green wood for the back logs to reflect the warmth of the fire into the lean-to.

Caution: To protect against the danger of fire, re-cover the lean-to with fresh green boughs each year.

BACK LOG FIRE

Bent-Pole Hut

- Four saplings growing in a square formation or four poles 12'–14' long and thin enough to bend
- One ridge pole about 2" in diameter and two feet longer than the sides of the hut
- Two door posts about 6' long and 2" in diameter
- About 40 crosspieces long enough to reach from one corner post to another and 1"–1½" in diameter
- About 40 shorter crosspieces cut to fit on the ends of the hut
- Plastic tarps to cover the top and ends of the hut
- Rope or wire for lashing
- Construction adhesive
- Evergreen boughs for thatching

The bent-pole hut, as the name implies, is made by bending poles to cross at the top, tying them together, and securing them with a ridge pole. This hut is relatively easy to make and can be built by one person. It costs very little, the only expense being plastic tarp and wire. The hut blends in well with the countryside because of its natural covering.

If you can't find four saplings growing in position as the plans suggest, cut them separately in the woods, bringing them to your building site. Thinning overgrown wooded areas can be healthy and beneficial for the taller and stronger trees. By burying the butt ends, 1½' into the ground, you can bend the poles in the same manner as you would the saplings.

Construction

1. If you look long and hard enough, you should be able to find four thin saplings growing in a square formation about 8′ apart. Bend them over and cut off the tops.

2. Lash the tops together and place a ridge pole into the V formed by the joint.

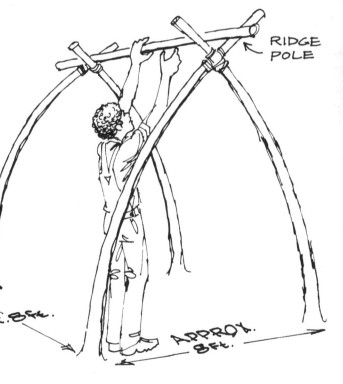

RIDGE POLE

APPROX. 8 ft.

APPROX. 8 ft.

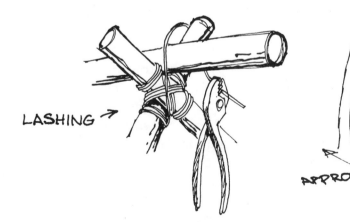

LASHING →

Lash together. Rope will do, but wire is longer lasting.
Make the ridge pole longer than the hut, as it will come in handy
to hang things on when you are finished.

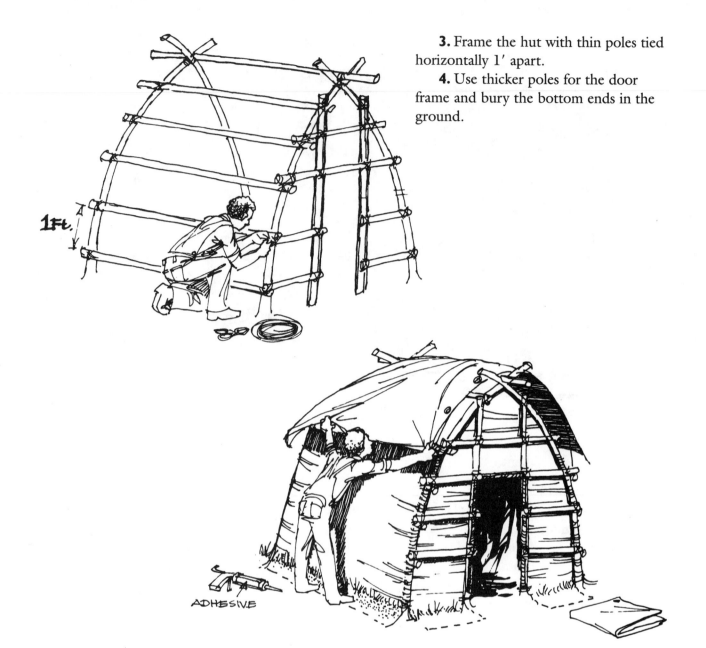

3. Frame the hut with thin poles tied horizontally 1′ apart.

4. Use thicker poles for the door frame and bury the bottom ends in the ground.

1 Ft.

ADHESIVE

5. Lay plastic tarp over the structure. Use a caulking gun to apply a good grade of construction adhesive to the poles. Seal the edges by wrapping the tarp around the glued poles and stapling the edges.

6. Dig a trench and run the edge of the tarp into the ground as a water barrier.

7. Cover the bottom edge with sod.

8. On the front and back of the hut, wrap the plastic around the poles from the inside.

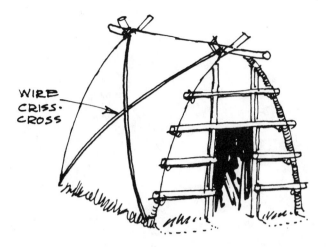

WIRE CRISS-CROSS

9. In order to strengthen the structure against high winds, criss-cross two wires on each side and secure them to the frame.

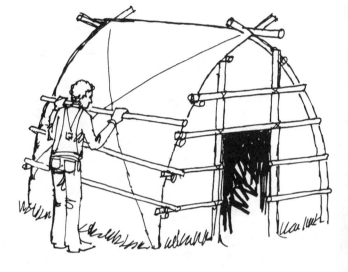

10. Lash additional poles along the sides, spacing them halfway between the poles that are underneath the plastic tarps. If you run out of straight poles, you can use 1⅜″ × ¼″ lattice.

11. Camouflage your hut with twigs, branches, grasses or whatever is handy. The best coverings are white pine boughs, which you can recognize by their long, soft needles, or balsam boughs, which are wonderfully fragrant. Cut the boughs 2′ long and hang them on the outside poles facing down, starting from the bottom and "shingling" up.

Adirondack Lean-To

In the early 1900s, it became fashionable, especially for the very wealthy, to camp out in the woods. Woodsmen were employed to build structures that would protect their occupants from wind and rain, while remaining open enough for their occupants to enjoy the great outdoors. The Adirondack lean-to was the perfect design. The wide opening at the front of the lean-to lets in plenty of fresh air and allows a reflector-style fire to penetrate and warm the interior space at night. At the same time, the broad overhang of the roof protects campers from unwelcome elements, like rain or snow. The design quickly caught on, and many examples of this structure can be seen across the country in recreational parks and camp sites.

Part	Quantity	Description
▶ **Logs**		
Base logs	2	About 12"-diameter, 14' long
Bottom side logs	2	10"–12"-diameter, 12' long
Side logs	22	About 8"-diameter, ranging in length from 5'–10'
Back logs	6	About 8"-diameter, 14' long
Side posts	2	Made from an 8"-diameter log, about 5' long, split lengthwise
Ridge pole	1	About 9"-diameter, 14' long
Roof support beams	2	About 9"-diameter, 14' long
Front rafters	10	4"-diameter, 6' long
Rear rafters	10	4"-diameter, 10' long
Roof boards	22	16' long, 1x6
Other materials	3 rolls	30 lb. roofing felt, 2 squares
		24" cedar shakes
		10" spikes
		6" nails
		Roofing nails

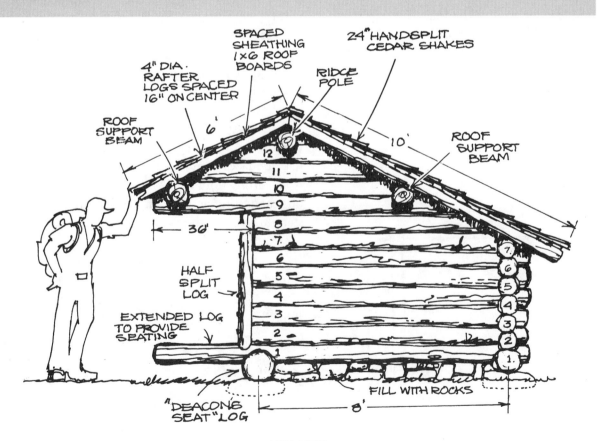

SIDE VIEW

Preparation

Before building the lean-to, peel the bark off the logs as described on page 18.

Select a campsite that has a beautiful view, but more importantly, faces away from the prevailing wind. If possible, face the lean-to southeast, so the sun's rays can awaken you in the morning and continue to warm the lean-to all day.

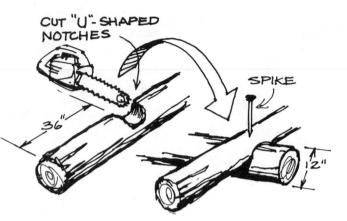

Foundation

1. Clear and stake out an area 12'×14'. Measure the diagonals, making sure they are of equal length. Lay large flat stones at each corner to serve as a foundation.

2. Select the largest log (approximately 12″ in diameter) to use at the base of the open front of the lean-to. This log is called the "Deacon's seat" and will provide a place for campers to sit while eating their meals. Lay a similar base log across the back side.

3. Complete the base of the lean-to, using two 10″–12″diameter logs for the bottom sides. Use a chain saw to cut ∪-shaped notches near the ends of the side logs so they will fit over the front and back logs, "Lincoln log" style. Every time you join two logs, hammer a 10″ spike through the center of the notched joint.

4. Fill the space underneath the bottom side logs with rocks.

Walls

1. Before continuing with the sides of the lean-to, split a straight 5′ log in half to make two vertical supports for the side logs to butt up against. Start splitting it with two metal wedges, then insert wooden wedges that you make on the site. Proceed, pounding in wedges in a straight line until the log splits.

2. Remove any bulges on the flat side of the log, using an ax. Do this by securing the log to the ground with pegs, positioning it so that the flat side faces away from you, preventing the ax from hitting your leg. This method is less dangerous than using an adze and straddling the log or standing on the log as the pioneers used to do.

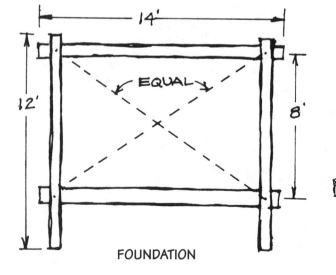

FOUNDATION

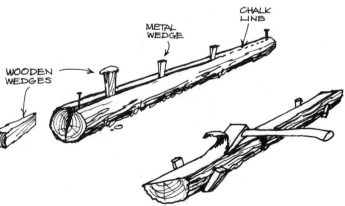

3. While building up the walls, install the vertical half-logs at each side of the front opening. As you continue building up the walls, check each course to make sure it is plumb with the preceding one. Secure the front ends of the logs by nailing through the vertical half-logs and into the front ends of the horizontal side logs. To help keep the courses level, reverse the larger butt ends of the logs as you go up.

4. After you lay the seventh rear wall log, the side logs will no longer be of uniform length because of the slope of the roof. The two "ninth" side logs support the front and rear roof beams, so make sure the logs extend 36″ beyond the lower logs at the front of the lean-to.

Roof

1. Cut two 9″-diameter, 14′-long support logs and install them across the structure on top of side logs #9. Add the top courses (logs 10, 11, and 12) and finish the roof framing with a ridge pole, using the straightest log you can find.

2. Snap a chalk line and cut off the ends of the top six logs on the side walls, cutting at an angle so there is a straight line running from the ridge pole to the front support beam and the rear wall beam (log #7).

3. Nail the rafter poles to the roof support beams, spacing the rafters 16″ on center.

4. There are several types of roofing material you can use — plywood, tar paper, rolled roofing, etc. — but the best looking by far is hand-split cedar shakes, which will give your lean-to the most authentic look. Cover the rafters with boards, spaced 4½″ apart, and nail shakes to the boards after covering them with a layer of 30 lb. felt. (See page 18 on "Roofs"). Constructed this way, the roof should last 20 to 30 years, without a drop of rainwater entering the shelter.

Build bunk beds inside, using 3″-diameter poles and 1×6 boards. Leave room under the bunks to store gear. This open shelter should comfortably accommodate four grown people.

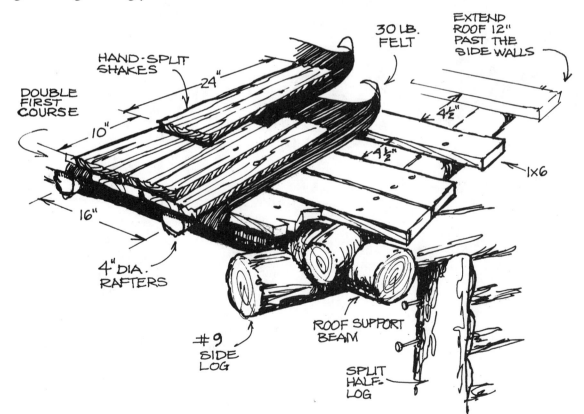

Bark Pyramid Hut

A pyramid hut will last a long time by virtue of its innate structural characteristics — just look at the ancient Egyptian tombs built for royalty. It seems to be perfectly balanced, with its square base and four sloping triangular sides meeting at the top. Some people believe that the pyramidal shape has mystical properties and an aura that preserves matter and increases longevity.

This pyramid is made with logs and covered with bark; however, it could also be made using 2×4s and covered with other materials such as boards, shingles, canvas, etc.

Part	Quantity	Description
Corner poles	4	12' long, 8"-diameter at the butt end
▶ *Door*		
Braces	2	6' long, 3"-diameter, forked at one end
Vertical supports	2	6' long, 3"-diameter
Side poles	2	3'–4' long, 3"-diameter
Crossbeams	2	6' long, 3"-diameter
▶ *Windows*		
Crossbeam	1 per window	3"-diameter, cut to fit at the preferred height
Supports	2 per window	1'–2' long, 3"-diameter, forked at one end
Side poles	2 per window	3"-diameter, about 1' long
Cross-branches	As needed	2"-diameter, various lengths ranging from 12' to less than 1'
Other materials		30 lb. felt
		Bark siding
		Mosquito netting or plastic sheets
		Wire or rope
		Nails

Frame

1. Select four straight 12' long poles and peel off the bark. Lash them loosely together at the top.

2. Clear and level a 12'-square area and set up the four poles.

POLES 8" IN DIAMETER AT BUTT ENDS

12 FT.

12 FT.

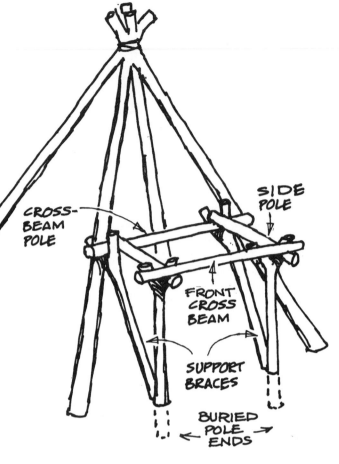

CROSS-BEAM POLE

SIDE POLE

FRONT CROSS BEAM

SUPPORT BRACES

BURIED POLE ENDS

3" DIA. POLES

CORNER POST

window opening

WIRE

NOTCH

DETAIL

3. About halfway up the front poles, attach a crossbeam supported by two forked braces.

4. Bury the ends of two more forked poles just in front of the supporting braces. The forked tops of these poles should be a little lower than the crossbeam attached to the pyramid frame.

5. Add two side poles. One end of each side pole will rest on the crossbeam, and the other end will rest in the fork of the vertical support pole. Put a front crossbeam pole over the ends of the two side poles and tie in place.

6. Windows can be made by framing out the sides. Cover the opening with mosquito netting, or use clear plastic sheeting if you are building in a cold climate.

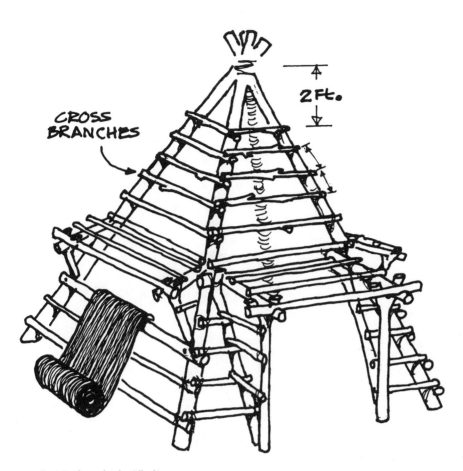

7. Nail or lash 2″-diameter cross branches to the corner posts, with 5″ spaces between branches.

Sides

1. If your hut is not too far from civilization, carry a roll of 30 lb. saturated felt (tar paper) to the site and cover the sides with it, stapling the tar paper to the cross branches. Cover the entire structure except for the top 2 feet, which should be left open for ventilation.

2. Cover the sides with bark, cut from dead trees. Start the cut with a saw and peel the bark off, using a long knife. Nail the bark slabs to the cross branches, beginning at the base and working up, in the same manner as shingling.

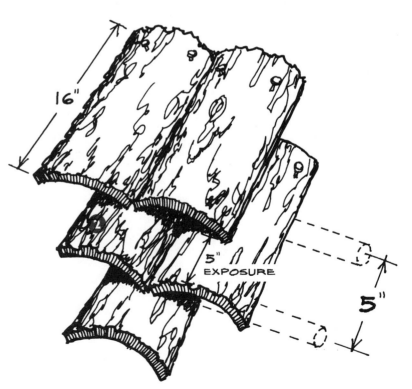

Hillside Hut

Perhaps you know of a hilly spot in the countryside, perhaps even near an old railroad line where you could have a load of used railroad ties dropped. This hillside hut requires approximately 70 of them. The floors and roof boards are made out of 2×6 pressure-treated wood, and 6″- to 8″-diameter logs serve as rafters to hold the roof boards. Use a chain saw to cut the railroad ties, and plan on replacing the chain when you are finished.

Part	Quantity	Description
▶ *Foundation and floor*		
Ground cover	1	6-mil plastic sheet, 12′ square
Floor beams	6	Railroad ties
Ledger boards	2	2x4, 8′6″ long
Floor boards	20	Pressure-treated 2x6, about 8′6″ long
▶ *Walls*		
Wall timbers	56	Railroad ties
Posts	3	Railroad ties
Braces	2	Railroad ties
Brace pegs	4	1¼″ hardwood dowels, about 10″ long
Plastic sheeting	As needed	
▶ *Window*		
Frame pieces	4	2x10, cut to fit opening
Center post	1	Made from two pieces of 1x4
Sashes	2	⅛″ Plexiglas sandwiched between two pieces of ½″ plywood
Shutters	2	Made from 1x6 boards backed by 1x4 braces
▶ *Roof*		
Rafters	7	6″-diameter logs, 10′ long
Baffle boards	12	2x6 boards, 1′ long
Roof boards	22	Pressure-treated 2x6, 10′ long
Plastic sheets	2	6-mil plastic, 10′ square
Roofing tar	As needed	
Roll roofing	One roll	
Sod	As needed	
Other material		One bag of cement and one cubic yard of sand for mortar
		Window and door hardware
		10″ spikes
		6″ nails
		Other assorted nails and screws
		Caulk

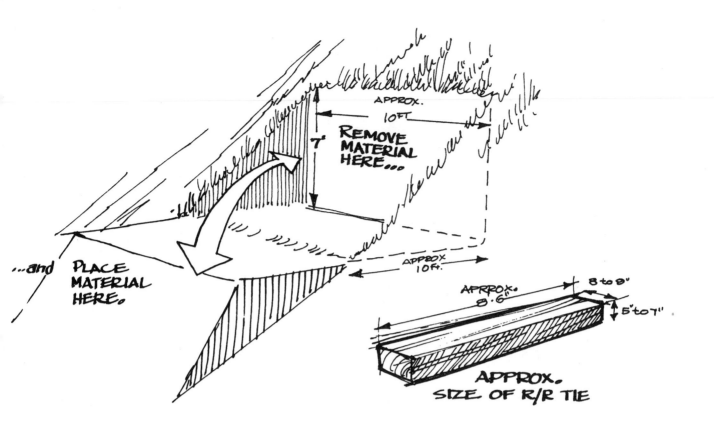

APPROX. 10FT

7'

REMOVE MATERIAL HERE...

...and PLACE MATERIAL HERE.

APPROX 10FT.

APPROX. 8·6"

8 to 9"

5 to 7"

APPROX. SIZE OF R/R TIE

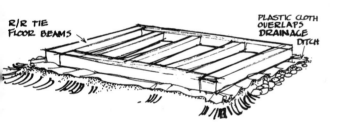

R/R TIE FLOOR BEAMS

PLASTIC CLOTH OVERLAPS DRAINAGE DITCH

Foundation and Floor

1. Begin by excavating the side of the hill. This is best done with a pick and shovel, burly arms and a strong back. Throw the excavated material to the front or low side of the hill so that it becomes the base to a level platform.

2. Dig a drainage ditch around the perimeter of your building (approximately 9′×9′), fill with loose rocks, and cover with a plastic ground cloth.

3. Lay floor beams on top of the ground cloth.

4. Nail ledger boards to the inside edge of the two end beams to support the ends of the floor boards.

5. Measure between the end beams and cut the floor boards to fit. Nail the boards to the floor beams and ledger boards.

Walls

1. Lap the ends of the ties alternately at the corners at the rear of the hut. To keep the ties from shifting, drive each one down onto two large nails embedded in the ends of the ties below. To do this, use a bolt cutter to cut off the heads of the nails after you have driven them halfway into the lower log with a sledge hammer.

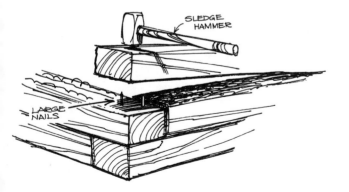

SLEDGE HAMMER

LARGE NAILS

WALLS

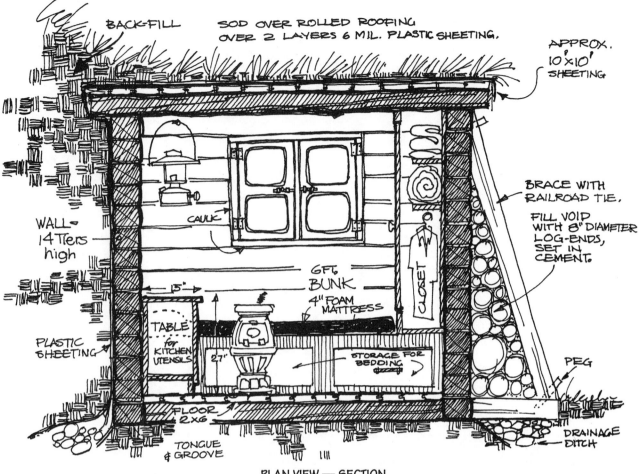

BACK-FILL

SOD OVER ROLLED ROOFING OVER 2 LAYERS 6 MIL. PLASTIC SHEETING.

APPROX. 10'×10' SHEETING

WALL 14 Tiers high

CAULK

BRACE WITH RAILROAD TIE.

FILL VOID WITH 8" DIAMETER LOG-ENDS, SET IN CEMENT.

6Ft. BUNK

4" FOAM MATTRESS

CLOSET

PLASTIC SHEETING

15'

TABLE for KITCHEN UTENSILS

27"

STORAGE FOR BEDDING

PEG

FLOOR 2×6

TONGUE & GROOVE

DRAINAGE DITCH

PLAN VIEW — SECTION

2. To ensure a watertight fit for the railroad-tie walls, mix 3 parts sand and 1 part cement into a loose, wet consistency. Lay the mortar down in two rows on top of each railroad tie before placing another tie on top. Remove any excess mortar and strike each joint with a 1″-diameter dowel or a piece of pipe.

3. The three posts at the front of the hut are railroad ties standing on end. Predrill holes in the posts and nail them to the ends of the abutting wall ties with 10″ spikes.

4. Set the window frame in place when the walls reach the right height for the sill, then continue building the walls around it.

5. Cut off the tops of the three posts before you put down the last tier of wall ties. Drill through the wall ties above the posts and drive a spike into the top of each post.

6. Reinforce the front wall with a railroad-tie brace at each corner. Fill the space between the brace and the wall with log ends set in cement.

7. Before backfilling around the back and side walls, cover them below grade with 6-mil plastic sheeting.

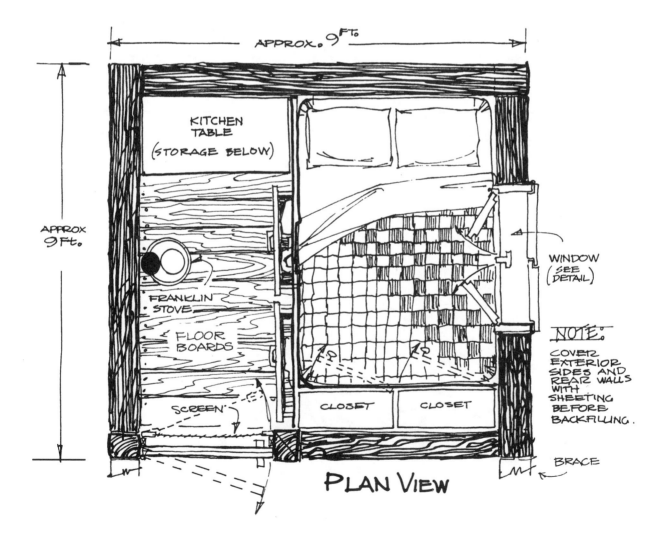

APPROX. 9 Ft.

APPROX 9 Ft.

KITCHEN TABLE
(STORAGE BELOW)

FRANKLIN STOVE

FLOOR BOARDS

SCREEN

CLOSET   CLOSET

WINDOW
(SEE DETAIL)

NOTE:
COVER EXTERIOR SIDES AND REAR WALLS WITH SHEETING BEFORE BACKFILLING.

BRACE

PLAN VIEW

Windows and Door

1. Make a center post for the window frame and nail it in place.

2. Cut front and back panels for the windows from ½″ plywood. Make the panel that faces the outside ½″ smaller on every side, but the hinge side, to provide a weather seal.

3. Cut out the window openings with an electric jig saw.

4. Sandwich a sheet of ⅛″ Lexan or Plexiglas between the plywood panels. Drill holes and screw the pieces together.

5. Mount the windows on the window frame hinged to open in.

6. Make security shutters as shown and mount them on the outside of the window frame.

7. Make a Dutch door (see information on doors on page 15) and hang it on the corner post so it swings out.

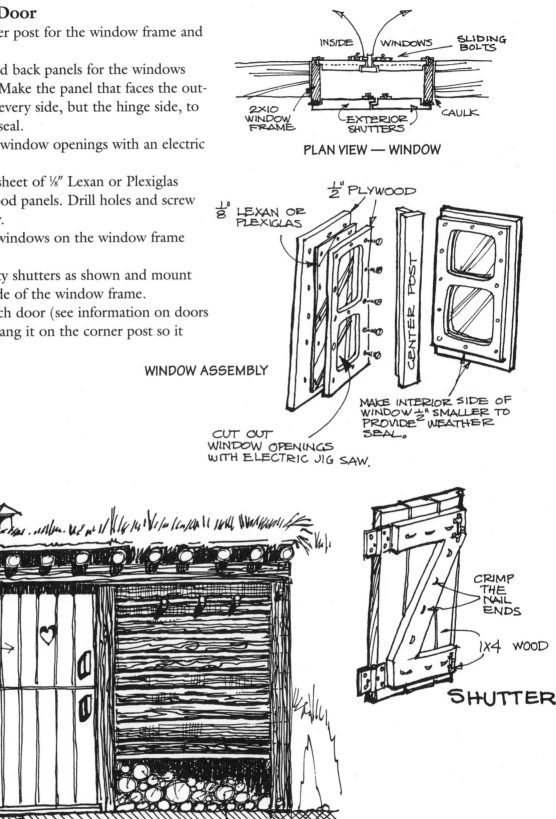

PLAN VIEW — WINDOW

WINDOW ASSEMBLY

⅛″ LEXAN OR PLEXIGLAS

½″ PLYWOOD

CENTER POST

MAKE INTERIOR SIDE OF WINDOW ½″ SMALLER TO PROVIDE WEATHER SEAL.

CUT OUT WINDOW OPENINGS WITH ELECTRIC JIG SAW.

INSIDE   WINDOWS   SLIDING BOLTS

2X10 WINDOW FRAME   EXTERIOR SHUTTERS   CAULK

1½″ THICK DUTCH DOOR, WITH SCREEN DOOR OPENING IN.

FRONT VIEW

FIREWOOD STORED UNDER BENCH

CRIMP THE NAIL ENDS

1X4 WOOD

SHUTTER

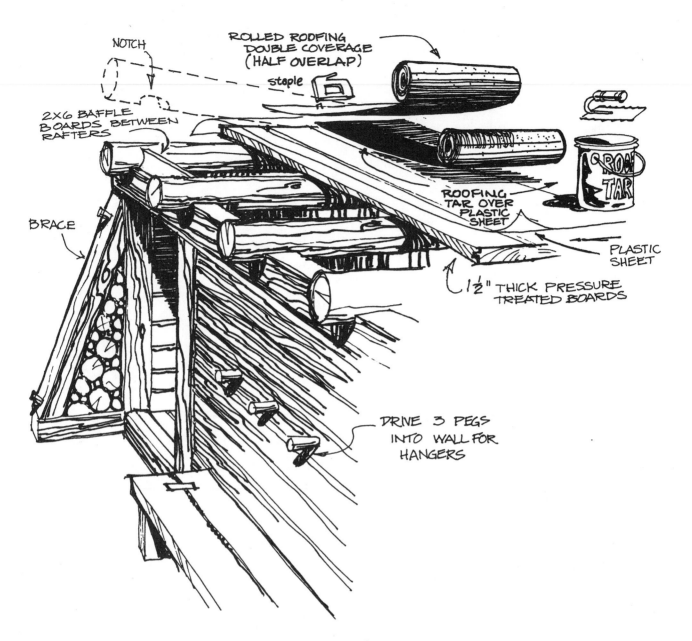

NOTCH

ROLLED ROOFING
DOUBLE COVERAGE
(HALF OVERLAP)

staple

2X6 BAFFLE
BOARDS BETWEEN
RAFTERS

ROOFING
TAR OVER
PLASTIC
SHEET

GROW
TAR

BRACE

PLASTIC
SHEET

1½" THICK PRESSURE
TREATED BOARDS

DRIVE 3 PEGS
INTO WALL FOR
HANGERS

Roof

1. Place the rafters 1′ apart, notching them to fit over the walls so their tops are level. Use 2×6 baffle boards to fill the spaces between them.

2. Lay roof boards over the rafters. Cover the boards with two layers of plastic sheeting followed by a coat of roofing tar and double-coverage rolled roofing.

3. Finally, cover the roof with sod (see information on sod roofs on page 19).

Sauna Hut

This retreat can serve as both a sauna and a weekend cabin. Ideally, a sauna is situated near a lake or stream into which the bathers can jump at the end of the bath. While they are swimming, the doors of the sauna are left open so the room can dry out and cool off, making it comfortable for overnight sleeping. In the winter, when our pond freezes, we use our sauna as a warming hut after ice skating, heating hot chocolate or mulled cider on top of the stove.

There are countless variations in designs of saunas, some even being underground. This one is raised on stilts to afford a better lake view from the deck. One thing most saunas have in common is excellence in carpentry and workmanship. To build a good sauna, one should not be hurried and should enjoy the process of building as much as the finished product.

This table shows the materials you need to build the shell of the sauna house. Finish features such as wall paneling, flooring, and furnishings will depend on your taste and your budget.

Part	Quantity	Description
▶ **Frame**		
Corner posts	4	14' 4x4 redwood
Corner post sheathing	8	14' 1x4 redwood
	8	14' 1x6 redwood
Top side beams	4	10' 2x10 fir
Top crossbeams	5	12' 2x10 fir
Bottom side beams	4	12' 2x10 fir
Bottom crossbeams	6	12' 2x10 fir
Braces	4	4' 4x4
▶ **Floor**		
Joists	7	12' 2x8
Flooring	3	4x8 sheets of ¾" plywood
▶ **Walls**		
Studs	30	2x4s ranging in length from 6'–8'7"
Misc. framing	As needed	2x4 cut to fit openings for windows, doors, stove
Sheathing	9	4'x8' sheets of ⅝" texture 1-11 plywood
Insulation		3½" fiberglass insulation
▶ **Roof**		
Rafters	5	12' 2x8
Roof deck	3	4'x8' sheets ¾" exterior plywood
Edge strips	2	12' 1x4
Cant strips	3	12' 2x4
Fascia	3	12' 1x4 redwood
Drip strip	1	12' long
Roll roofing	1 roll	36"-wide double coverage (mineral surface)
▶ **Railing**		
Posts	3	42" 2x4
Side rails	2	5' 1x4
Front rail	1	12' 1x4
Other material	1	Window
	2	Doors
	16	½"x5½" bolts
	4	½"x7" bolts
		1¼" dowel for pegs
		Wood preservative
		Cement
		Silicone caulk
		Glue
		Woodstove

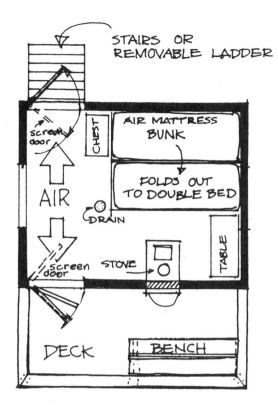

STAIRS OR
REMOVABLE LADDER

screen door

CHEST

AIR MATTRESS
BUNK

FOLDS OUT
TO DOUBLE BED

AIR

DRAIN

Screen door

STOVE

TABLE

DECK

BENCH

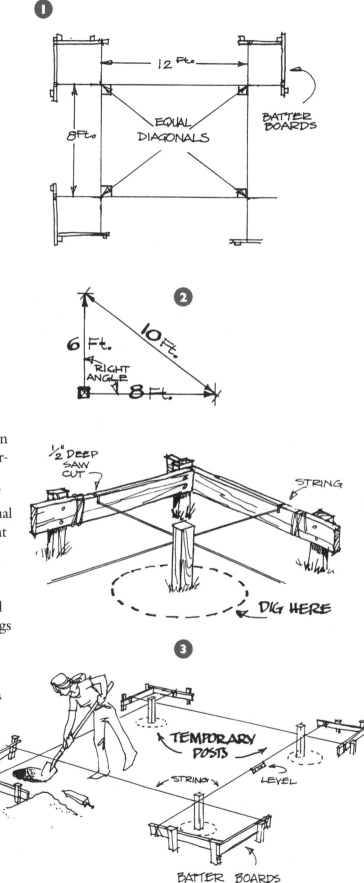

Site Preparation

1. Begin by measuring and laying out the position of the four posts, setting up batter boards at each corner and adjusting strings to measure 8′ and 12′.

2. Use the Pythagorean Theorem — the sum of the squares of the two sides of a right triangle is equal to the square of the hypotenuse — to make sure that the strings are at right angles where they intersect. Measure 6′ from the corner along one string and mark that point. Measure 8′ from the corner along the other string and mark that point. If the diagonal distance between the two points is 10 feet, the strings are at a right angle and the corner is square.

3. Drive a temporary post in each corner, double checking the accuracy of their positions by carefully measuring the diagonals, which should be equal. After you are sure the strings are square and accurate, make a ½″-deep saw cut where each string is attached in the top of the batter board and remove the post. The string can be replaced any time to double check the position of the post.

(4)

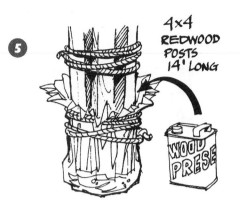

(5)

4×4 REDWOOD POSTS 14' LONG

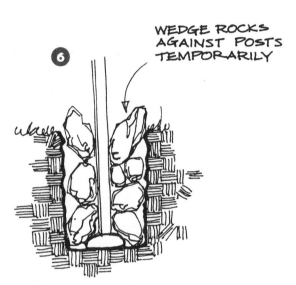

(6)

WEDGE ROCKS AGAINST POSTS TEMPORARILY

4. Dig a hole in each corner, 18″ in diameter and 4′ deep.

5. To protect the posts against rot, wrap a heavy plastic bag or sheet around the bottom of each one. Fill the bag with preservative and allow to soak for three days.

6. Place a large flat rock at the bottom of each hole underneath the post so water will drain off. Place the posts in the holes and wedge rocks against them to hold them in place temporarily, in case any adjustments have to be made later.

7. When the frame is finished and the sheathing has been nailed to the posts, fill the holes with a cement/sand mixture and stones.

8. As the wood shrinks away from the cement, a crack will appear. Caulk this every year.

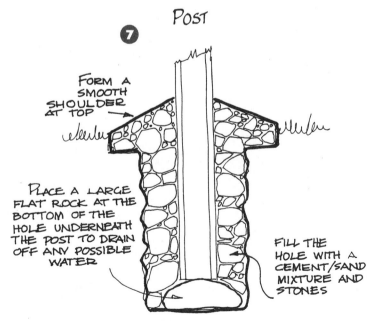

POST

(7)

FORM A SMOOTH SHOULDER AT TOP

PLACE A LARGE FLAT ROCK AT THE BOTTOM OF THE HOLE UNDERNEATH THE POST TO DRAIN OFF ANY POSSIBLE WATER

FILL THE HOLE WITH A CEMENT/SAND MIXTURE AND STONES

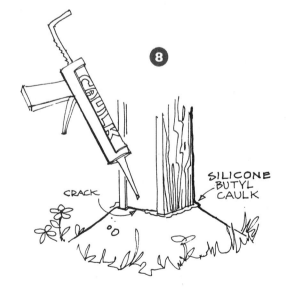

(8)

CRACK

SILICONE BUTYL CAULK

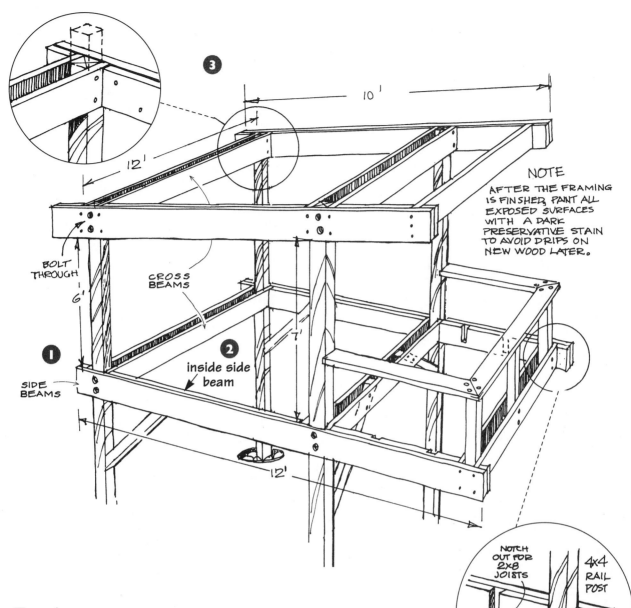

10'

12'

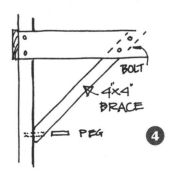

NOTE
AFTER THE FRAMING IS FINISHED, PAINT ALL EXPOSED SURFACES WITH A DARK PRESERVATIVE STAIN TO AVOID DRIPS ON NEW WOOD LATER.

BOLT THROUGH

6'

CROSS BEAMS

7'

inside side beam

SIDE BEAMS

12'

NOTCH OUT FOR 2×8 JOISTS

4×4 RAIL POST

2×10

8"

BOLT

4×4 BRACE

PEG

Framing

1. Nail the lower crossbeams to the corner posts, then bolt the outside side beams to the posts. Repeat this procedure for the upper crossbeams and outside side beams.

2. Cut the inside side beams to fit between the crossbeams and nail them in place. Before inserting the sections under the deck, cut notches for the two deck joists.

3. Cut off the tops of the corner posts after the beams are attached.

4. Cut the ends of the corner braces at a 45° angle. Put the braces in place against the corner posts and between the crossbeams. Drill holes and bolt the braces to the beams and peg them to the posts.

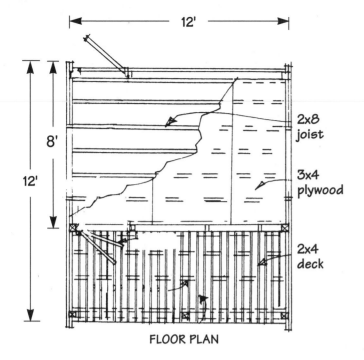

FLOOR PLAN

12'

8'

12'

2x8 joist

3x4 plywood

2x4 deck

5. Nail and bolt the three 2×4 posts for the deck railing between the front crossbeams.

6. After the heavy framing is finished, paint all exposed surfaces with a preservative stain to avoid drips on new wood later on.

Floor

1. Attach floor joists to the lower side beams every 16″ on center. The two joists under the deck are supported by the notches you cut in the inside side beam. The five joists under the sauna are supported by metal joist hangers.

2. Nail ¾″ exterior plywood to the joists for the sauna floor.

3. Nail or peg 2×4 planks to the deck joists.

Walls

1. Frame the walls with 2×4 studs placed 16″ on center. Studs are sandwiched between the crossbeam at the front and rear of the sauna, making a strong connection between the floor and roof.

2. Frame the openings for the window, doors, and stove. The stove opening should allow 8″ clearance around the stove on all sides.

3. Nail the plywood siding to the studs.

4. Cover the corner posts beneath the building with redwood sheathing.

5. Install the railing for the deck. For an extra touch of elegance, use the corner detail shown on page 75.

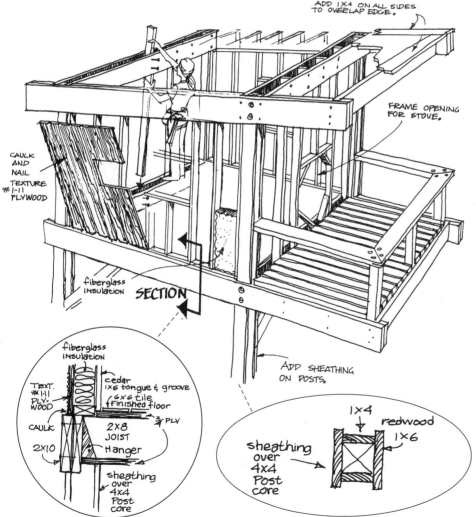

ADD 1X4 ON ALL SIDES TO OVERLAP EDGE.

FRAME OPENING FOR STOVE.

CAULK AND NAIL TEXTURE #I-11 PLYWOOD

fiberglass insulation

SECTION

ADD SHEATHING ON POSTS.

fiberglass insulation

TEXT. #1-11 PLY-WOOD

CAULK

2x10

cedar 1x6 tongue & groove

6x6 tile finished floor

3 PLY

2x8 JOIST

Hanger

sheathing over 4x4 post core

sheathing over 4x4 post core

1x4

redwood 1x6

If you want to show off your carpentry skills, this corner detail is a good place to do it. Not only is it a handsome joint, it is also extremely strong.

1. Cut the ends of the railing pieces at a 45° angle and cut slots in the end 2" deep and ⅜" wide.

2. Put the railing pieces together to make a 90° angle. Join them with a 4"-wide plywood chevron glued into the slot where they meet.

3. Drill ¾" holes through the railing pieces and the plywood chevron.

4. Make pegs to fill the holes from a ¾" hardwood dowel. Cut slots in both ends of the pegs.

5. Cut wedges from the end of a piece of hardwood.

6. Tap wedges a little way into the slots at both ends of the peg. Insert the peg into the hole and then tap the wedges all the way in. This will expand the peg and keep it from falling out.

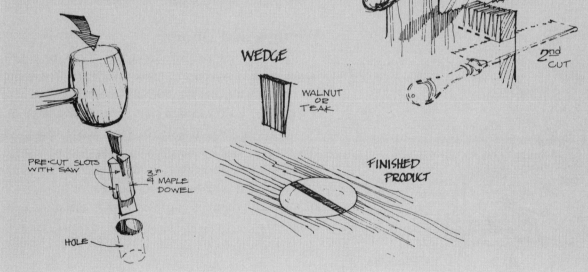

Roof

1. Hang the roof joists from the side beams every 16" on center, using metal joist hangers.

2. Nail ¾" exterior plywood to the joists, leaving the tops of the outside side beams exposed. Screw 1x4 strips to the tops of the side beams to extend the roof so it has a 2" overhang on the sides.

3. Bevel one edge of the 2x4 cant strips to 45°. Nail the cant strips to the edge of the roof along the front and sides.

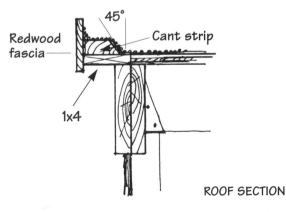

ROOF SECTION

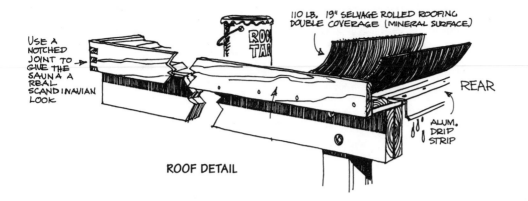

USE A NOTCHED JOINT TO GIVE THE SAUNA A REAL SCANDINAVIAN LOOK

110 LB. 19" SELVAGE ROLLED ROOFING DOUBLE COVERAGE (MINERAL SURFACE)

ROOF TAR

REAR

ALUM. DRIP STRIP

ROOF DETAIL

4. Nail a redwood fascia to the cant strips to finish the edges of the roof. Use notched joints at the corners of the fascia to give the sauna a real Scandinavian look.

5. The facia is left off the rear of the roof so water can drain off. Finish this edge with an aluminum drip strip.

6. Cover the roof with two layers of roll roofing.

Window and Doors

You can buy used windows and doors for your sauna, house, or you can make your own. You'll find instructions for making both in Chapter 2. But here is another window design that has the advantage of being double insulated. If you have access to a table saw with a dado blade, you can make this window frame at home and easily assemble it at the building site. The same molding design serves for head, jamb, and sill. The frame is cut from two 8′ pieces of 2×6 redwood.

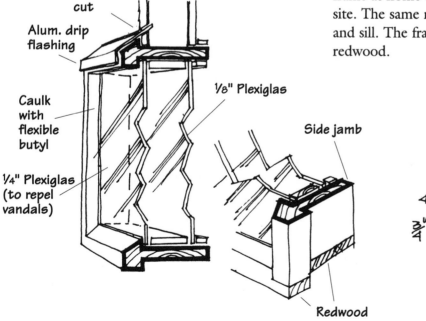

Kerf saw cut

Alum. drip flashing

Caulk with flexible butyl

1/4" Plexiglas (to repel vandals)

1/8" Plexiglas

Side jamb

Redwood

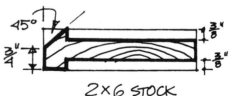

45°

3/8"

3/4"

3/8"

2×6 STOCK

Stove

The stove extends through the wall of the sauna so it can be fed from outside. After you set it in place in the wall opening, fill in the space around it with brick and mortar. Check local fire codes to make certain your installation meets all requirements for clearances and materials.

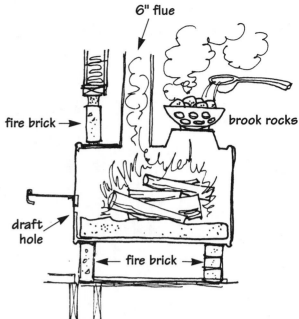

6" flue

fire brick →

brook rocks

draft hole

← fire brick →

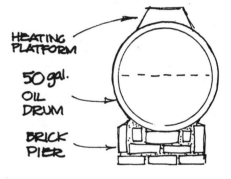

HEATING PLATFORM

50 gal. OIL DRUM

BRICK PIER

Ivy-Covered Grow Hut

This hut is built with a framework of thin lattice strips, covered with a nylon parachute and chicken wire and planted with ivy, clematis, or any fast-growing, climbing vine. It can be built in a weekend by two people and blends in beautifully with the environment. This is a lightweight hut, and the building materials can be easily carried far back into the woods.

Part	Quantity	Description
Pegs	6	1x2, 1′ long
Arches	12	1⅜″ lattice, 16′ long
Strengtheners	2	1⅜″ lattice, 14′ long
Expansion pieces	3	1⅜″ lattice, 4′ long
Door ridge piece	1	1⅜″ lattice, 18″ long
Door arches	2	1⅜″ lattice, 6′ long
Cover	1	Used parachute
Skylight frame pieces	6	1x3, 3′6″ long
Skylight dome pieces	3	1⅜″ lattice, 4′ long
Other material		Chicken wire
		8-mil plastic sheeting
		Hinges
		Waterproof glue
		Silicone waterproofing
		String or wire
		Zipper

Preparing the Arches

1. Divide the twelve pieces of 16′ lattice into six pairs.

2. Glue the pairs together and, while the glue is still wet, bend each pair into an arch approximately 8′3″ from end to end.

3. Allow the arches to dry in this position.

4. Separate the six pairs of arches when they are dry, and you will find that they will keep their shape.

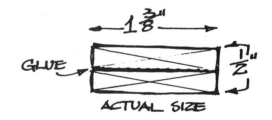

GLUE →

1⅜″

½″

ACTUAL SIZE

LATTICE STRIP

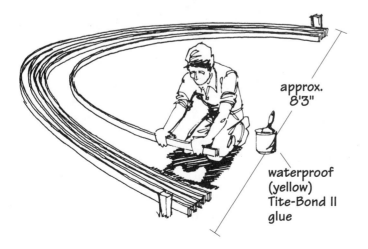

approx. 8′3″

waterproof (yellow) Tite-Bond II glue

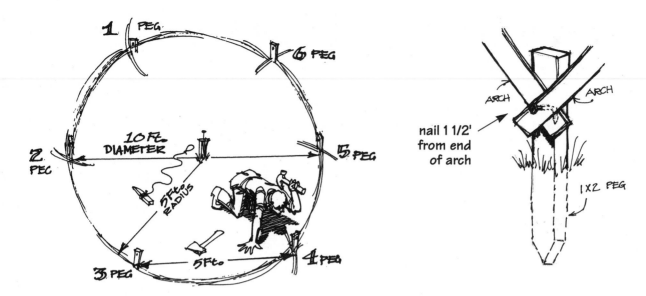

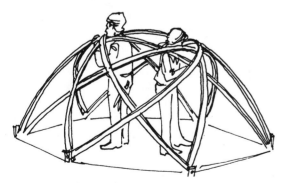

Framing

1. Find a site that seems particularly adaptable to growing plants. Scribe a 10′-diameter circle, using a pointed stick and string.

2. Using the same compass string and the same radius of the circle, mark off six points at equal distances around the circumference of the circle. Hammer in a 1×2 peg at each point.

3. Pre-drill holes 1½″ from arch ends.

4. Assemble the six arches so that each end lies at a peg. As you go around the circle, attach one end of an arch to peg 1 and the other end to peg 3. Attach the next arch to peg 2 and peg 4. Continue in the same manner until all six arches are attached. The arches are secured by pushing a nail through pre-drilled holes in both arch ends and in the pegs. Bend the nail over to hold it in place.

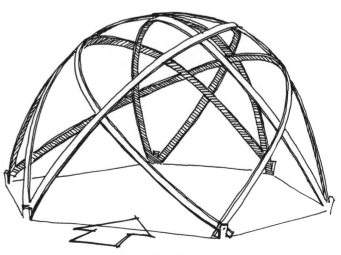

ERECTED FRAMEWORK

5. From the center, lift up the arches gradually, working together until the arches form a hexagonal-shaped opening overhead — just like opening an umbrella!

6. Adjust the lattice strips by eye, tying them temporarily, until you have a hexagonal opening at the top, approximately 3½' across.

7. When the arches look consistent, lash the junctions diagonally and across with strong hemp string or wire. You'll be surprised how quickly the framework becomes strong as you continue to lash the joints.

temporary

permanent

lash together using string or wire

4' expansion pieces

8. Attach three pieces of lattice, 4' long, to make expansion pieces across the hexagonal opening at the top. Bow them up in the center and nail them securely at the ends. Then lash the three pieces together at the center.

9. Add 14' strengtheners to the sides, wiring or tying them to the frame and pegs.

10. Bend the two door arches so the tops of the arches are at the same height as the top of the door opening. Nail the arches to the strengtheners near the bottom of the door opening.

11. Drill holes in the ridge piece. Cut 1⅜" notches as shown. Put string or wire through the holes and lash the ridge piece to the door arches.

14' strengtheners

frame for roof over doorway

ridge piece

notch

DOOR ENTRANCE

Covering the Hut

1. Cover the frame with a parachute, purchased at an Army/Navy surplus store.

2. Optional: Cut a hole in the top and place a clear plastic skylight over it. Make the skylight out of 1×3 lumber joined to form a hexagonal frame. Bend lattice strips inside the frame to form a dome and cover with two layers of 8-mil plastic sheeting stapled to the inside of the frame. Place the skylight in position and attach it to the frame of the hut with hinges. Waterproof the parachute by covering with one coat of Silicone water repellent or exterior vinyl paint (any color).

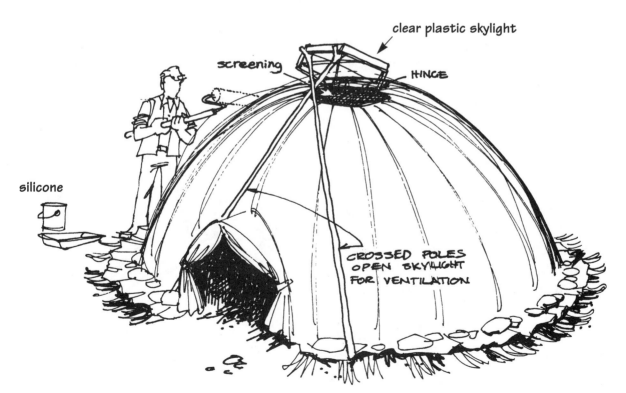

clear plastic skylight

screening

HINGE

silicone

CROSSED POLES OPEN SKYLIGHT FOR VENTILATION

chicken wire

3. Place rocks over the edges to weigh down the parachute.

4. Cut the parachute down the center where it falls over the door and sew in a zipper. Use Velcro strips for curtain tie-backs.

5. Backfill around the grow hut with good soil.

6. Wrap 24″-wide chicken wire over the entire structure and tie overlapping layers together for strength and to hold vines in place.

7. Plant ivy or any other fast-growing vine. Wild clematis or jasmine also work well and have fragrant blossoms in the spring.

CHAPTER 5

On the Water

We said there warn't no home like a raft, after all.
Other places do seem so cramped up and smothery, but a raft don't.
You feel mighty free and easy and comfortable on a raft.

Mark Twain, *Huckleberry Finn*

River Raft

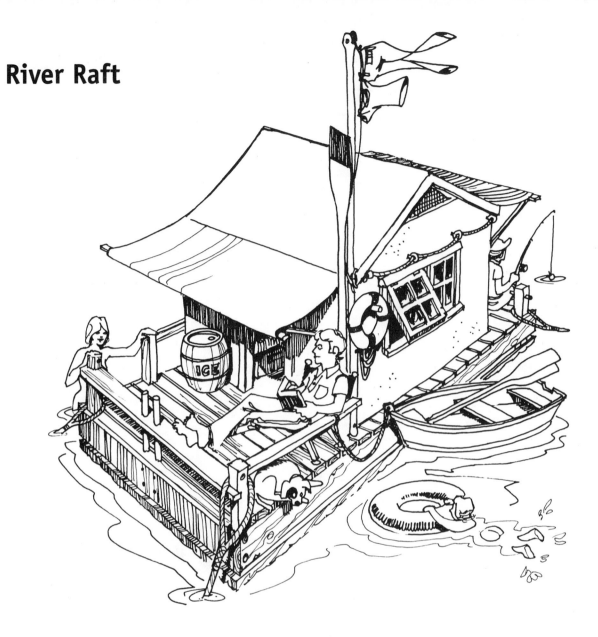

More sophisticated than Huckleberry Finn's log raft, this river raft would have made Huck's life much easier. Using basic raft construction, with boards resting on top of foam billets, this type of raft is often used in lakes and at camps as a floating dock and diving platform. A rope across the stern end of the raft keeps the oar secure, yet can be easily removed when you are moored so you can sit on the bench. Build a simple cabin on top of the decking, and the raft becomes an inexpensive summer home, avoiding taxes and a steep mortgage. Either arrange to have your floating home towed to a fantastic, isolated spot each summer, or set yourself adrift and float downstream. If you want to be more mobile, mount two outboard motors to the stern and motor down the river.

Part	Quantity	Description
▶ *Deck*		
Corner posts	4	4' 4x4
Skirt Boards	2	12' 2x10
	2	8' 2x10
	2	12' 2x6
	2	8' 2x6
Crossties	4	8' 2x6
Skids	3	12' 2x6
Bracing	2	12' 2x10
	2	8' 2x10
Billets	6	54" long, 7"x20"
▶ *Floats*		
Decking	24	8' 2x6
Bench	1	8' 2x10
Steering posts	2	2½"-diameter posts, 4' long
Side posts	2	4' 4x4
Railing	1	4' 2x4
▶ *Cabin*		
Wall framing	About 30	7' 2x3
Rafters	8	4' 2x3
Ridge pole	1	7' 2x3
Ridge posts	2	21" 2x3
Floor	2	4'x8' sheets of ⅛" hardboard
Sheathing and roofing	8	4'x8' sheets ½" Homasote
Awning		Canvas, 8' wide and 13' long
Awning props	2	3' 1x2
Awning rods	2	7' 1x2
Other materials	28	½"x6" carriage bolts and washers
	12	½"x11" galvanized carriage bolts
	4	⅜"x5" bolts
		2½" galvanized deck screws
		Enamel paint
		Windows with hardware
		Screen door with hardware
		Assorted galvanized nails
		Bronze staples
		¾" cotton rope

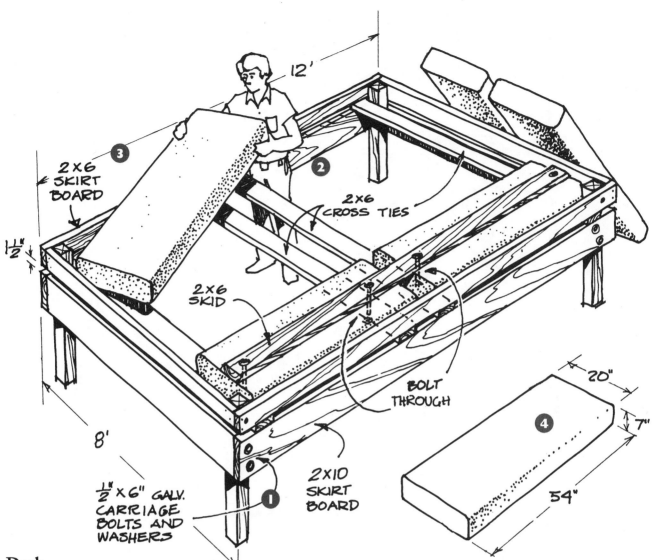

12'

③ **2×6 SKIRT BOARD**

② **2×6 CROSS TIES**

$1\frac{1}{2}$"

2×6 SKID

BOLT THROUGH

8'

20"

7"

④

54"

$\frac{1}{2}$" × 6" GALV. CARRIAGE BOLTS AND WASHERS

① **2×10 SKIRT BOARD**

Deck

1. Begin by building the raft upside-down (as shown in the illustration above). Use pressure-treated lumber for the frame. Bolt the 2×10 skirt boards onto the corner posts.

2. Nail the 2×6 crossties on top of the 2×10 skirt boards.

3. Bolt the four 2×6 skirt boards to the corner posts, resting them on the ends of the crossties. (The crossties are sandwiched between the 2×6 and 2×10 skirt boards.)

4. Put the six foam billets in place. Lay one 2×6 skid board on top of each pair of billets.

5. Drill four ½"-diameter holes through each skid board, continuing the hole through the billet and into the crossties. Insert a ½"×11" galvanized carriage bolt (a total of twelve) through the holes, attaching a washer and nut underneath each one.

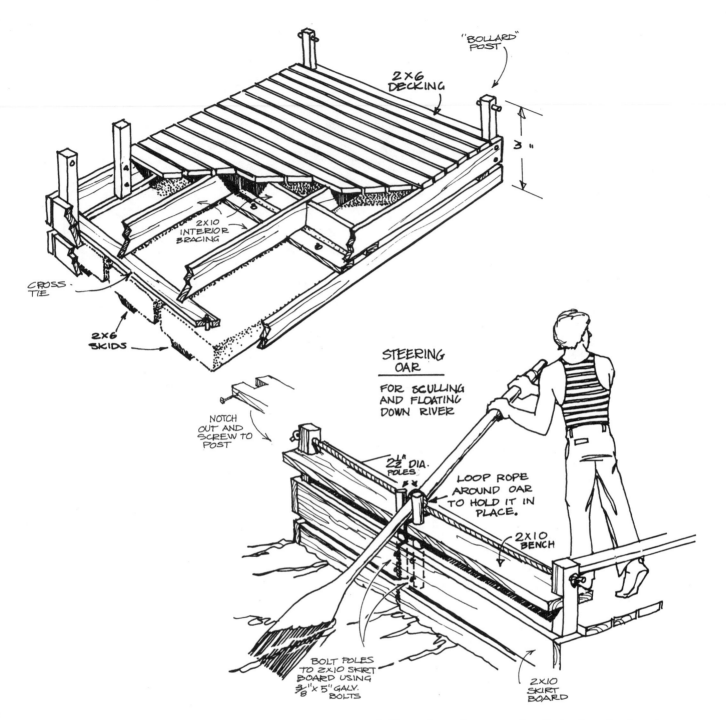

"BOLLARD" POST

2×6 DECKING

3"

2×10 INTERIOR BRACING

CROSS TIE

2×6 SKIDS

NOTCH OUT AND SCREW TO POST

STEERING OAR

FOR SCULLING AND FLOATING DOWN RIVER

2½" DIA. POLES

LOOP ROPE AROUND OAR TO HOLD IT IN PLACE.

2×10 BENCH

BOLT POLES TO 2×10 SKIRT BOARD USING ⅜"×5" GALV. BOLTS

2×10 SKIRT BOARD

6. Turn the raft over and nail the interior bracing in place.

7. Bolt steering posts to the 2×10 skirt board, using ⅜"×5" galvanized bolts. Also bolt the two 4×4 rail posts to the 2×10 skirt board.

8. Nail on the decking, using galvanized nails.

9. Make a bench by notching out each end of a 2×10 board to fit around the corner posts and drilling two holes for the steering posts. The bench sits on two blocks cut from a 2×4 and screwed to the corner posts.

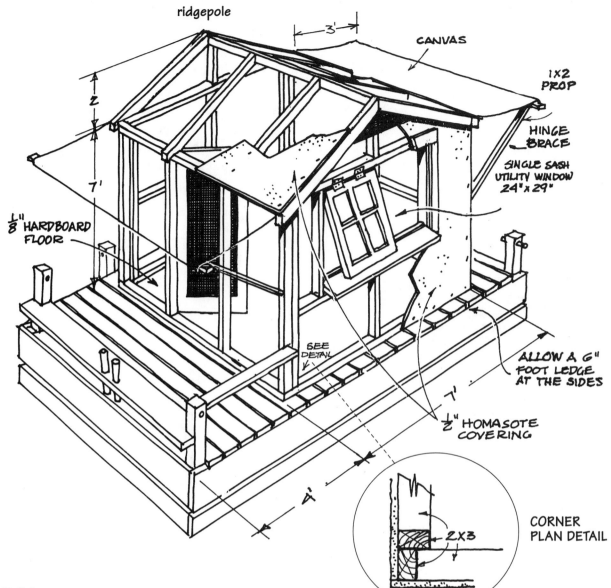

ridgepole

CANVAS

3'

2'

7'

1×2 PROP

HINGE BRACE

SINGLE SASH UTILITY WINDOW 24" x 29"

$\frac{1}{8}$" HARDBOARD FLOOR

SEE DETAIL

ALLOW A 6" FOOT LEDGE AT THE SIDES

7'

$\frac{1}{2}$" HOMASOTE COVERING

4'

2X3

CORNER PLAN DETAIL

Cabin

The lightweight cabin is built out of 2×3 framing lumber and is sheathed with ½" Homasote, which looks like grey cardboard.

1. Build each wall flat on the deck, then raise and join the walls, using 2½" deck screws.

2. Use 2×3s to frame the windows and the 30"-wide door opening.

3. Install a ridgepole supported by 2×3 posts, so the peak of the roof is 21" higher than the top of the walls.

4. Cut eight rafters, 4' long, with a 64° angle at the ridgepole end. Mark and cut a bird's mouth notch at the other end, where the rafters meet the outside edge of the wall. Screw the rafters on, using 2½" screws.

5. Cover the roof with Homasote, nailing 1½" roofing nails every 8". To waterproof the Homasote,

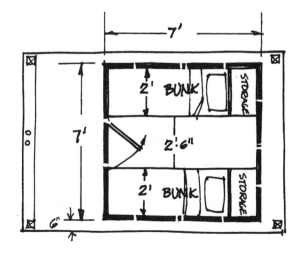

7'

2' BUNK STORAGE

7'

2'6"

2' BUNK STORAGE

6"

paint it with two coats of exterior enamel, making sure to paint the edges.

6. Cover the roof with canvas awning, folding it over the edges on the gable ends and stapling it to the underside of the roof with bronze staples. Allow the awning to extend 3′ beyond the edge of the roof on each side and staple the end to a 1×2 awning rod. Use 1×2 props to extend the awning over the deck.

7. Install windows and doors.

TRAILER CHASSIS CAPACITY 1500 Lbs.

The river raft can be transported on a low-bed trailer chassis. The raft will stick out from the sides by one foot and off the rear by four feet, but most of the weight should be directly over the wheels.

When not in use on the water, the raft can serve as a children's playhouse in your backyard.

Bon voyage!

Water Gazebo

If you are lucky enough to live on a lake or protected bay, this water gazebo provides a wonderful shelter, camping spot, and mooring and swimming dock, all in one. It is the perfect place to invite friends to tie up their boats and cool off after fishing or water skiing on a hot summer day.

Part	Quantity	Description
▶ *Platform*		
Frame pieces	6	16' 1×12
Supports	6	16' 1×12
Sheathing	16 panels	½" exterior plywood, 4'×8' panels
Skids	3	16' 2×4
▶ *Tower*		
Corner posts	4	8"-diameter logs, 12' long
Crosspieces	8	6"-diameter logs, 8' long
Braces	8	4"-diameter logs, 3' long
Center post	1	5"-diameter log, 16' long
Floor frame and joists	7	8' 2×6
Floor	16 pieces	Pressure-treated decking, 1¼"×6", 8' long
Rail	4	9' 2×4
Rail supports	8	9' 2×4
Siding	70 pieces	
	(186 linear feet)	1×6 tongue-and-groove cedar, 32" long
Roof		Custom-made canvas awning
Awning rods	4	8' 1×2
Awning props	8	3' 1×2
Ladder pole	1	4"-diameter log, 10' long
Ladder rungs	7	2"-diameter, 2' long
Other materials	16	5" angle irons
	4	4" angle irons
	16	½"×8" lag screws
	14	¼"×3½" lag screws
	6	Joist hangers
		Epoxy glue
		Fiberglass cloth
		Polyester resin
		2" stainless steel screws
		2½" stainless steel siding nails
		Mosquito netting

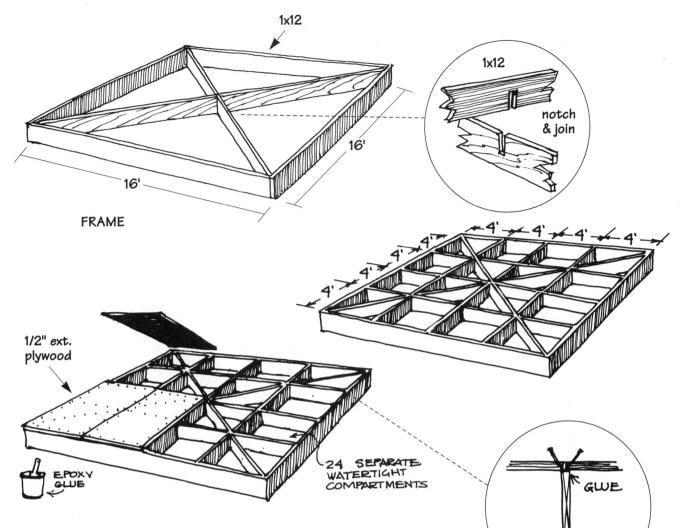

1x12

notch & join

FRAME

1x12

◄ 4' ► ◄ 4' ► ◄ 4' ► ◄ 4' ►

1/2" ext. plywood

EPOXY GLUE

24 SEPARATE WATERTIGHT COMPARTMENTS

GLUE

Platform

1. Begin by making a 16′×16′ frame out of 1×12 #2 pine near the water's edge. Construct four sides and two diagonal crosspieces (to keep the platform from racking).

2. Fill in the frame with additional 1×12 boards so there is a support every 4′.

3. Glue and nail ½″ exterior plywood over the frame. After the first side has cured, turn the platform over and repeat the same process on the second side. Caution: Epoxy gives off toxic fumes. Work outside with a respirator mask.

4. Cover all sides of the platform with two layers of fiberglass cloth soaked in polyester resin, which can be applied with a roller or a brush. (Wear long gloves when handling the cloth.) Cover the sides first, then overlap with the top covering.

5. Use epoxy to glue 2×4 skids to the bottom of the platform. Then drill 2″-long stainless steel screws through the skids and into the bottom of the platform every 2′.

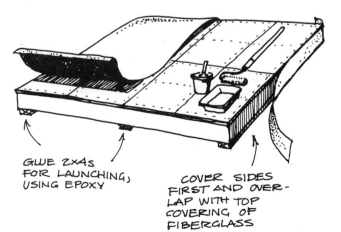

GLUE 2X4s FOR LAUNCHING, USING EPOXY

COVER SIDES FIRST AND OVERLAP WITH TOP COVERING OF FIBERGLASS

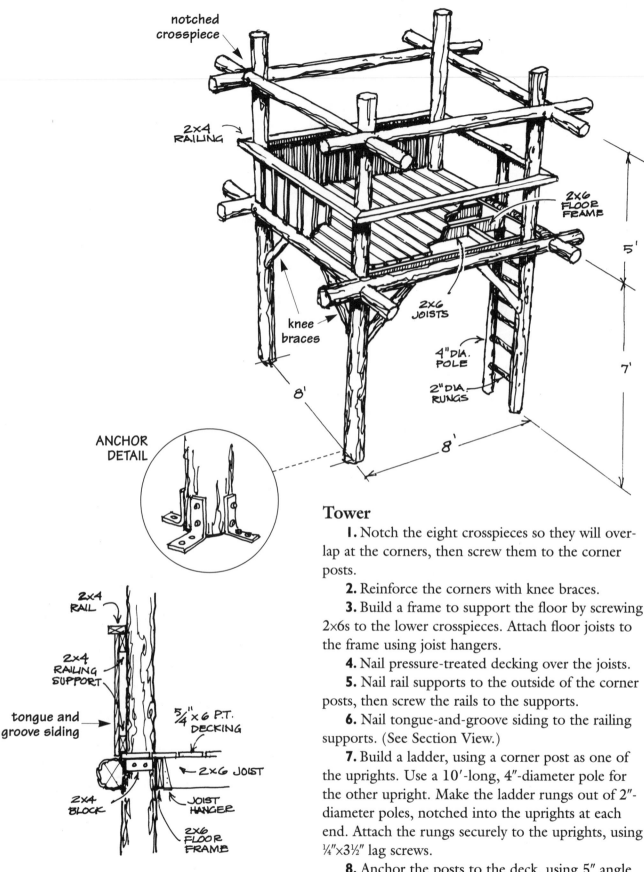

notched
crosspiece

2×4
RAILING

2×6
FLOOR
FRAME

knee
braces

2×6
JOISTS

5'

4" DIA.
POLE

2" DIA.
RUNGS

8'

7'

8'

ANCHOR
DETAIL

2×4
RAIL

2×4
RAILING
SUPPORT

tongue and
groove siding

5/4"×6 P.T.
DECKING

2×6 JOIST

2×4
BLOCK

JOIST
HANGER

2×6
FLOOR
FRAME

SECTION VIEW

Tower

1. Notch the eight crosspieces so they will over-lap at the corners, then screw them to the corner posts.

2. Reinforce the corners with knee braces.

3. Build a frame to support the floor by screwing 2×6s to the lower crosspieces. Attach floor joists to the frame using joist hangers.

4. Nail pressure-treated decking over the joists.

5. Nail rail supports to the outside of the corner posts, then screw the rails to the supports.

6. Nail tongue-and-groove siding to the railing supports. (See Section View.)

7. Build a ladder, using a corner post as one of the uprights. Use a 10'-long, 4"-diameter pole for the other upright. Make the ladder rungs out of 2"-diameter poles, notched into the uprights at each end. Attach the rungs securely to the uprights, using ¼"×3½" lag screws.

8. Anchor the posts to the deck, using 5" angle irons. (See Anchor Detail.)

9. Install the center post by securing it to the platform using four 4″ angle irons.

10. Take a drawing of the gazebo and the precise measurements of the top crosspieces and the center pole to an awning maker to have the roof made.

When the water gazebo is finished, gather a bunch of friends for a launching ceremony. Roll it to the water's edge on top of round logs, float it out to the desired location, and anchor it in place. If you don't have enough people to move the gazebo without mechanical assistance, rig a block and tackle from the platform frame to anchor it in the water and then to the trailer hitch of a truck.

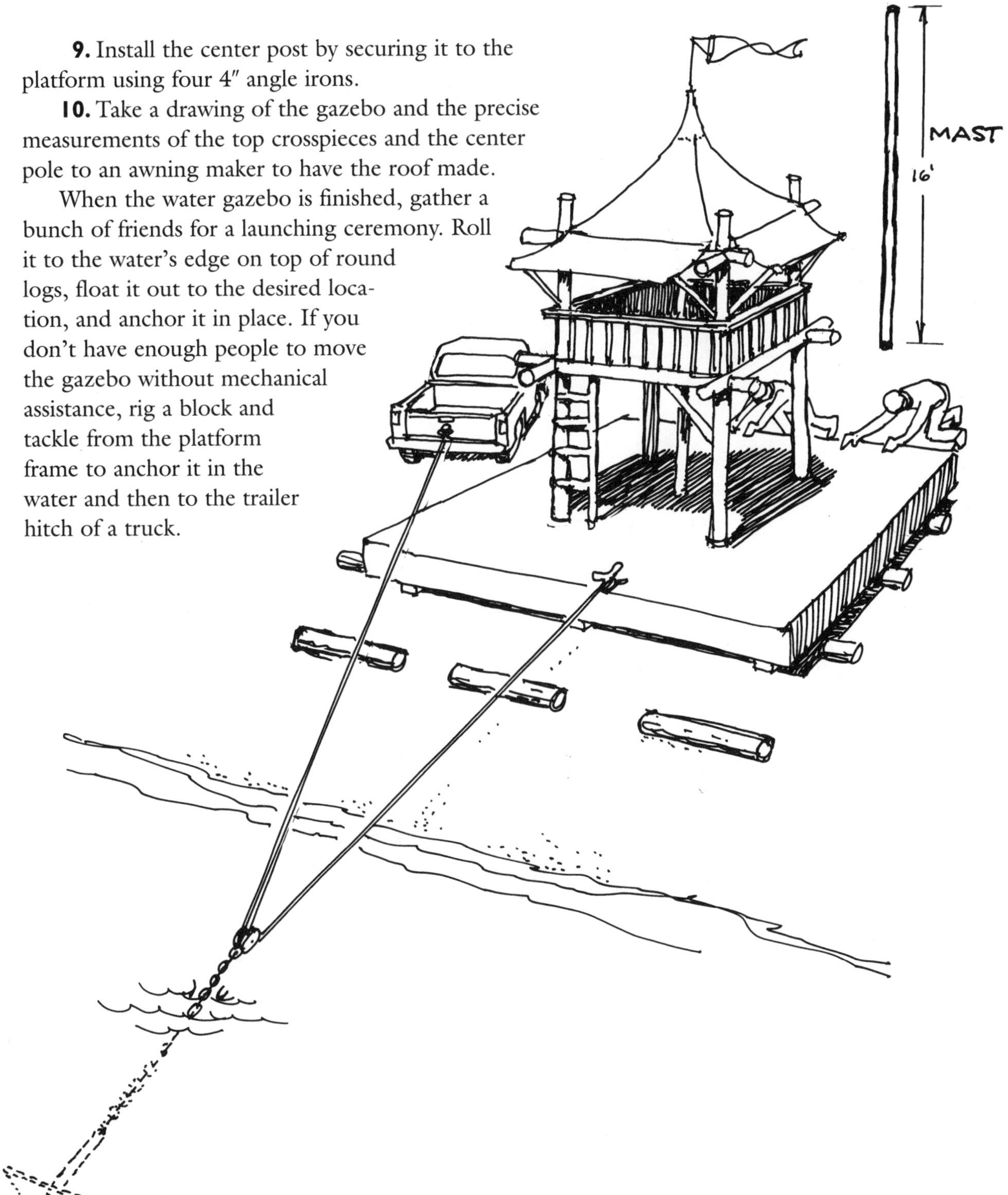

MAST

16'

CHAPTER 6

In the Trees

The branches spread out — high bridges over the earth. A slight breeze blew; the sun shone. . . . Everything seen from up there was different, which was fun in itself.

Italo Calvino, *The Baron in the Trees*

▶ Make safety your first consideration when building a tree house.

▶ If possible, make the first platform within arm's reach from the ground, or at least within reach of a stepladder. It is very difficult to climb a tree holding onto boards, hammers, and nails.

▶ Use a safety harness and make sure the rope from the harness is attached to a strong branch.

▶ Provide strong handles at the top of ladders and inside doorways to make climbing in and out of your tree house safer and easier.

▶ If you plan to use your tree house for several years, make sure the tree you build in is strong and sound.

▶ Allow for flexibility in the joints so the tree can grow and move with the wind.

▶ Use only galvanized nails. Unprotected nails will rust away in three years.

▶ For framing tree houses, galvanized deck screws are more practical to use than nails. Screws not only hold better, but they can also be removed if you need to modify or add on to your hut.

▶ For attaching beams, use ½"-diameter, galvanized hex-head lag screws with washers rather than relying on several little nails. A socket wrench is very handy for putting lag screws into wood.

▶ Materials particularly suitable for tree house construction are synthetic rope (not manila), steel cable, and forked branches (for braces).

▶ You can nail or screw into large trees without causing much damage, but never cut the bark all the way around the tree, as this will surely kill the tree.

▶ Don't worry if the frame of your tree house is not square; it is more important to make sure it is level.

▶ Use 2×6 braces where support is needed and branches do not exist.

▶ Check with your local lumber yard for knot-free scrap wood or ask a local builder for scrap wood from a new house site.

▶ Always take advantage of what the tree offers in the way of natural supports. Never design your tree hut first and then try to find a tree that fits. Let the tree suggest to you what the design should be.

Triangular Tree House

This particular tree house does not require the use of tree branches for its support. Instead, the hut is cantilevered off the tree trunk with the help of braces and cables. The structure's triangular, rather than rectangular, shape gives it greater strength.

You will need a tall ladder to build this structure and to enter it when you are finished. Hide the ladder in the woods to keep out unwelcome guests when you are not using the tree house.

Note: The lengths given for beams and braces are approximate.
They can vary depending on the size of the tree.

Part	Quantity	Description
▸ *Platform frame*		
Bottom side beams	2	8' 2x8
Crossbeams	3	2x8 approx. 8', 5', and 3' in length
Rear brace	1	3' 2x6
Front support braces	2	6' 2x6
▸ *Cabin*		
Floor	1½ panels	¾" exterior plywood
Top side beams	2	8' 2x8
Crossbeams	3	2x8 approx. 8', 5', and 3' in length
Wall studs	10	7' 2x4
Siding		Rough slab lumber
Roof	1½ panels	¾" exterior plywood
Roof trim	2	8' 1x2
Other materials	2	Turnbuckles
	2	¾"x4" lag screws
	2	½"x7" bolts with washers
	2	½"x3" bolts with washers
		¼" steel cable, 20' long
		1½"-diameter steel pipe as long as the diameter of the tree
		Roll roofing
		4" galvanized nails
		Other assorted nails and screws

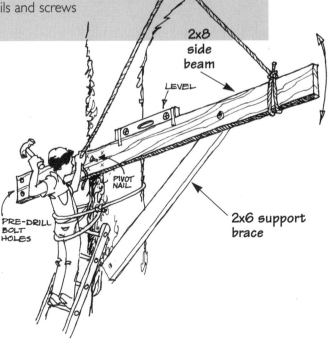

Platform Framing

1. Throw a rope over a branch, high up in the tree. Attach the loose end of the rope to one end of a 2x8 side beam and use the other end of the rope to hoist up the beam. Drive a pivot nail in the center of the beam where it joins the tree.

2. Pull on the loose end of the rope to level the beam and hammer in four 4"-long, galvanized nails or screws.

3. Attach a 2x6 support brace to the side beam and the tree to help hold the beam in place.

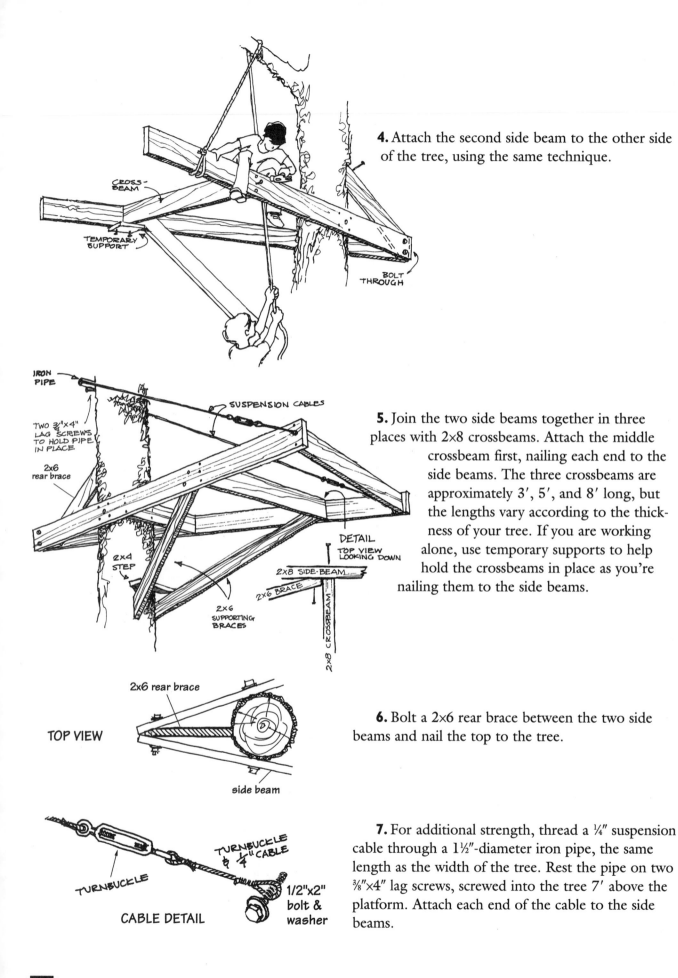

CROSS-
BEAM

TEMPORARY
SUPPORT

BOLT
THROUGH

4. Attach the second side beam to the other side of the tree, using the same technique.

IRON
PIPE

SUSPENSION CABLES

TWO ⅜"×4"
LAG SCREWS
TO HOLD PIPE
IN PLACE

2×6
rear brace

2×4
STEP

2×6
SUPPORTING
BRACES

DETAIL
TOP VIEW
LOOKING DOWN

2×8 SIDE-BEAM

2×6 BRACE

2×8 CROSSBEAM

5. Join the two side beams together in three places with 2×8 crossbeams. Attach the middle crossbeam first, nailing each end to the side beams. The three crossbeams are approximately 3′, 5′, and 8′ long, but the lengths vary according to the thickness of your tree. If you are working alone, use temporary supports to help hold the crossbeams in place as you're nailing them to the side beams.

2×6 rear brace

TOP VIEW

side beam

6. Bolt a 2×6 rear brace between the two side beams and nail the top to the tree.

TURNBUCKLE

TURNBUCKLE
& ¼" CABLE

¼" CABLE

1/2"×2"
bolt &
washer

CABLE DETAIL

7. For additional strength, thread a ¼" suspension cable through a 1½"-diameter iron pipe, the same length as the width of the tree. Rest the pipe on two ⅜"×4" lag screws, screwed into the tree 7′ above the platform. Attach each end of the cable to the side beams.

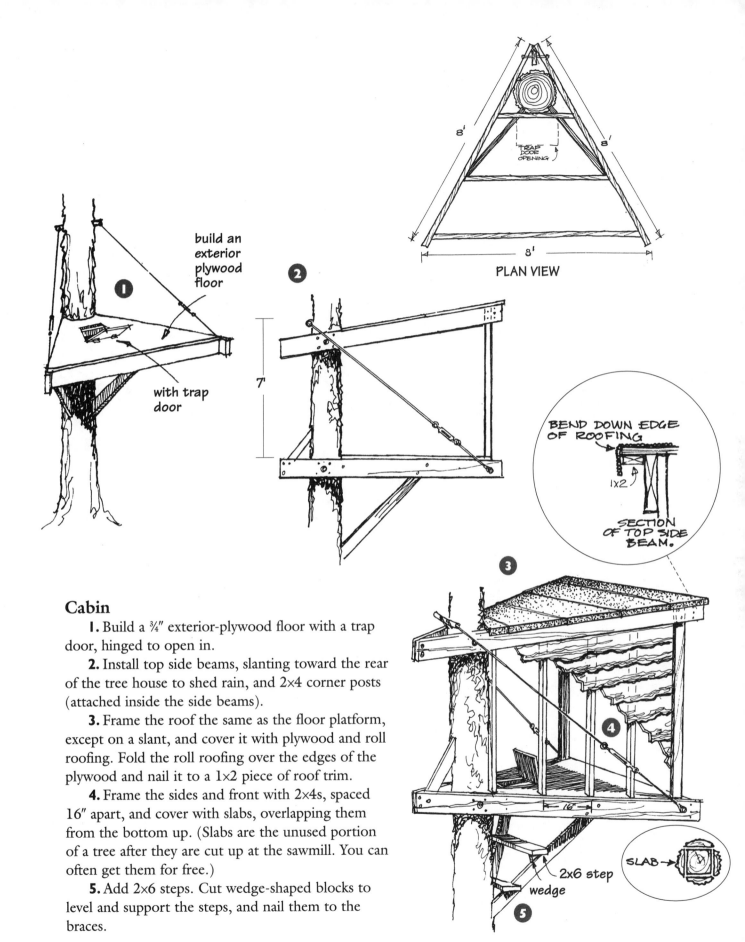

PLAN VIEW

build an
exterior
plywood
floor

with trap
door

BEND DOWN EDGE
OF ROOFING

SECTION
OF TOP SIDE
BEAM.

SLAB →

2x6 step
wedge

Cabin

1. Build a ¾″ exterior-plywood floor with a trap
door, hinged to open in.

2. Install top side beams, slanting toward the rear
of the tree house to shed rain, and 2×4 corner posts
(attached inside the side beams).

3. Frame the roof the same as the floor platform,
except on a slant, and cover it with plywood and roll
roofing. Fold the roll roofing over the edges of the
plywood and nail it to a 1×2 piece of roof trim.

4. Frame the sides and front with 2×4s, spaced
16″ apart, and cover with slabs, overlapping them
from the bottom up. (Slabs are the unused portion
of a tree after they are cut up at the sawmill. You can
often get them for free.)

5. Add 2×6 steps. Cut wedge-shaped blocks to
level and support the steps, and nail them to the
braces.

Fold-Up Tree House

This tree house can be locked up while you are away by folding down the front roof and lifting up the front deck. Although the hut shown here is built using cut lumber, it could just as well be made using logs and thatched with evergreen boughs or bark. The deck can be accessed by a rope ladder, as shown in the illustration, or by a makeshift ladder, which can be hidden in the woods nearby when not in use.

Note: The lengths of the beams and braces, and consequently the size of your tree house, will vary depending on the arrangement of the trees you are using. Find the trees first, then make a more exact list of the materials you will need.

Part	Quantity	Description
▶ *Platform*		
Bottom crossbeam	1	2x8
Bottom side beams	2	2x8
Ledge strips	2	1x2
Joists and bridging		2x6
Floor		¾" exterior plywood
Railing posts	2	4x4, 40" long
Railing	2	1⅝"-diameter poles
▶ *Cabin*		
Top crossbeam	1	2x4
Top side beams	2	2x8
Ledge strips	2	1x2
Joists and bridging		2x6
Roof		¾" exterior plywood
Fascia strips	4	1x2
Wall framing		2x4
Siding		1x6
Locking panels	2	¾" exterior plywood
Edge strips	4	1x4
Props	2	1x3
Other materials	10	½"x5" lag screws
	4	½"x6" bolts
	4	Hinges
	2	Locking hasps
		Rolled roofing
		Aluminum flashing
		½"-diameter rope

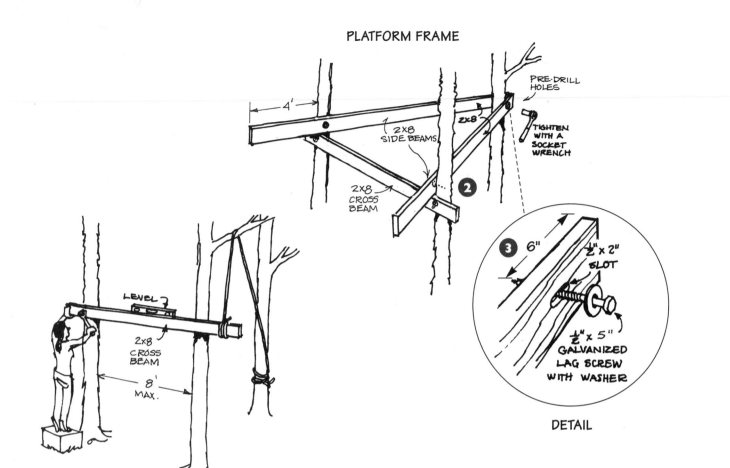

PLATFORM FRAME

4'

2x8 SIDE BEAMS

2x8

PRE-DRILL HOLES

TIGHTEN WITH A SOCKET WRENCH

2x8 CROSS BEAM

②

③ 6"

$\frac{1}{2}" \times 2"$ SLOT

$\frac{1}{2}" \times 5"$ GALVANIZED LAG SCREW WITH WASHER

DETAIL

LEVEL

2x8 CROSS BEAM

8' MAX.

CROSS SECTION

DETAIL

2x8

2x6 JOIST

1x2 LEDGE STRIP

4x4 post

1x2 ledge strip

2x6 floor joists

⑥

2x8 side beam

⑤

bridging

⑦

rasp

Framing

1. Select three strong, healthy trees growing in the right formation. Throw a rope over one of the upper branches, tie it to the end of the crossbeam, and use the other end of the rope to hoist the crossbeam up into the air and against a tree.

2. Attach the other end of the crossbeam to a second tree, and when the crossbeam is level, secure it to both trees using ½"×5" lag screws.

3. Drill two holes, 2" apart, about 6" from one end of each side beam. Chisel out the wood between the two holes to make a slot.

4. Using the crossbeam for support, attach the side beams to the rear tree using a ½"×5" lag screw inserted through the slot in each beam. (The slot will allow the beam to give with the movement of the trees.) The side beams should extend 4' past the two front trees.

As a general rule, it is better to use one large bolt or lag screw rather than a lot of small nails, which can rust through in a few years. As the tree grows in circumference, it may be necessary to back off the lag screws a few turns.

5. Nail a 1×2 ledge strip along the inside bottom edge of each side beam.

6. Cut floor joists out of 2×6 lumber and install them every 16″. Cut the ends of the joists at an angle to match the angle at the side beams.

7. As the span increases toward the front of the frame, add 2×6 bridging between the joists to strengthen the structure.

8. Cover the cabin floor joists with exterior plywood or 2×6 tongue-and-groove planks. Leave the porch uncovered.

9. Cut two pieces of 4×4 for the railing posts and shape the bottoms to fit inside the corners, using a rasp. Bolt the posts onto the side beams with ½″×6″ bolts.

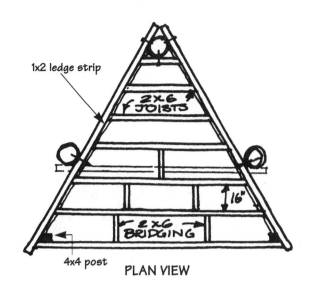

PLAN VIEW

Cabin

1. Attach the top crossbeam to the two front trees with ½″×5″ lag screws. The bottom of the crossbeam should be 7′ above the platform.

2. Cut slots in both ends of the top side beams and attach them to the front and rear trees with lag screws. Note that the top side beams go *under* the crossbeam. Slant the side beams so the roof is 7′ above the floor in the front and 4′ in the back.

3. Frame the cabin roof the same way you framed the floor, with ledge strips, joists, and bridging. Then sheath the roof with exterior plywood.

4. Cut two pieces of exterior plywood for the porch roof and deck floor panels. Reinforce the edges of both panels with 1×4s. Hinge the roof panel to the top crossbeam and the floor panel to the edge of the cabin floor so the two panels will fit together when folded. Attach locking hasps so you can secure the tree house when you are away.

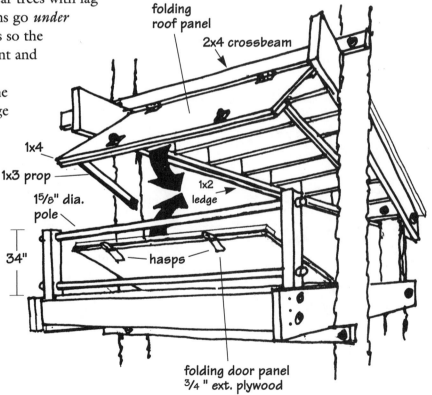

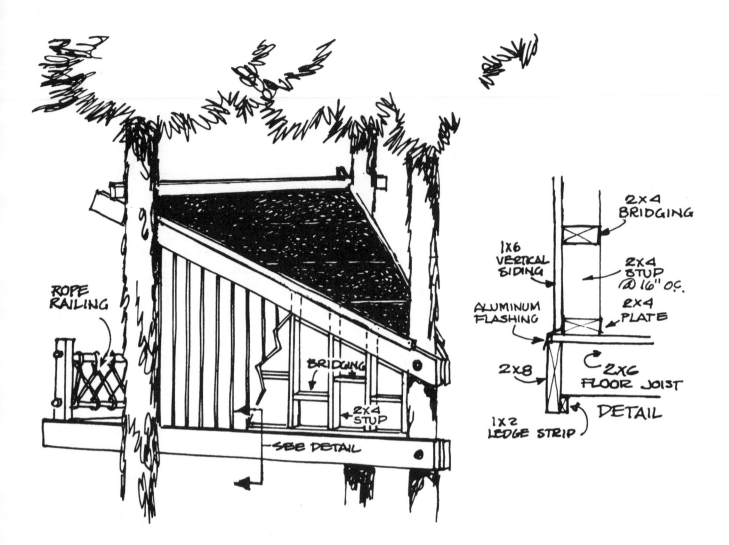

ROPE RAILING

BRIDGING

2×4 STUP

SEE DETAIL

1×6 VERTICAL SIDING

ALUMINUM FLASHING

2×8

1×2 LEDGE STRIP

2×4 BRIDGING

2×4 STUP @ 16" O.C.

2×4 PLATE

2×6 FLOOR JOIST

DETAIL

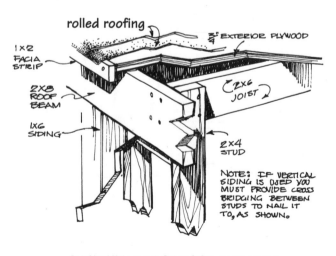

rolled roofing

3/4" EXTERIOR PLYWOOD

1×2 FACIA STRIP

2×8 ROOF BEAM

1×6 SIDING

2×6 JOIST

2×4 STUD

NOTE: IF VERTICAL SIDING IS USED YOU MUST PROVIDE CROSS BRIDGING BETWEEN STUDS TO NAIL IT TO, AS SHOWN.

CUTAWAY VIEW OF ROOF AND WALL

5. Drill holes in the rail posts and insert $1\frac{5}{8}$"-diameter rails. Weave ½"-diameter rope in a crisscross fashion to complete the railing.

6. Frame the walls using 2×4 studs every 16" on center. The bottom of each stud is nailed to a 2×4 plate, and the top is nailed to the side beam and a joist. Nail horizontal bridging between the studs to support the vertical siding. (See Detail.)

7. Install aluminum flashing along the edge of the floor, and nail the siding to the studs.

8. Attach a 1×2 fascia strip to the side edges of the plywood roof and cover the roof with two layers of rolled roofing. Use 36" tar paper, overlapping the layers by 12". Start at the low end and work up to the front.

9. Build in a combination bench/storage unit to store camping gear.

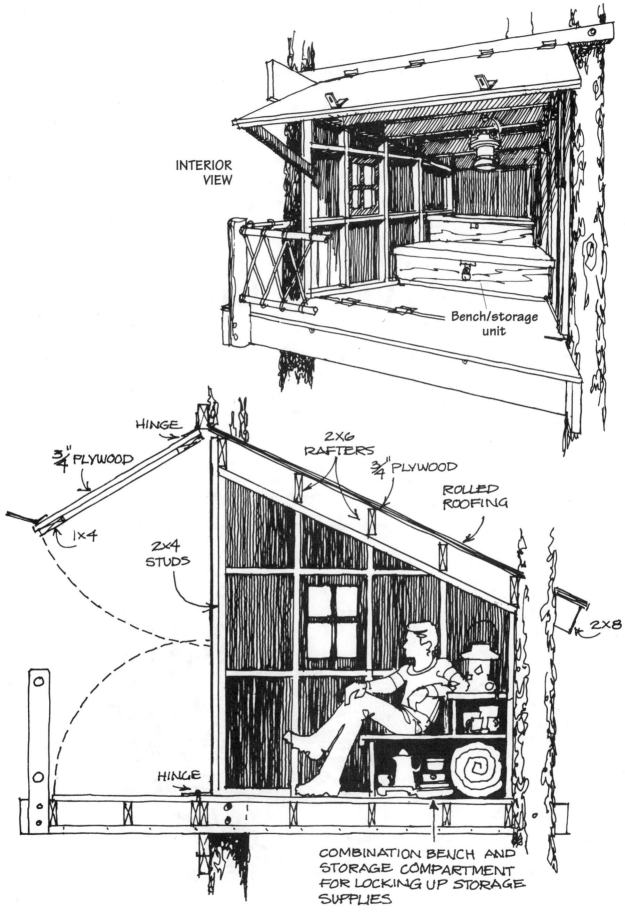

INTERIOR VIEW

Bench/storage unit

HINGE

3/4" PLYWOOD

2X6 RAFTERS

3/4" PLYWOOD

ROLLED ROOFING

1x4

2x4 STUDS

2X8

HINGE

COMBINATION BENCH AND STORAGE COMPARTMENT FOR LOCKING UP STORAGE SUPPLIES

SECTION VIEW

CHAPTER 7

Primitive Native Shelters

The term "architecture" refers to more than just the design and decoration of buildings.
It embraces what happens whenever human thought or action makes order and meaning of random space.

Peter Nabokov and Robert Easton, *Native American Architecture*

Wigwam

Ask the average person what type of shelter the American Indian lived in and he or she will probably answer "tipi" or "tepee"; however several Indian tribes, specifically the woodland Indians, built and lived in wigwams, a more permanent dwelling place than the tipi. The wigwam was constructed out of materials indigenous to the area in which the dwellers lived. Those who lived in northern wooded areas used saplings covered with birch bark, while those who lived in the plains, where buffalo were plentiful, used hides or reed mats to cover their wigwams. The dome-shaped wigwam is a warm, romantic shelter that blends in with the woods.

Materials Needed

- *Frame:* 28 saplings, 1" to 1½" in diameter, ranging from 10' to 16' long
- *Horizontal poles:* Made from thin, pliable saplings as needed
- *Green wood strips:* Made from split saplings or thin branches as needed
- *Cover:* Primed artist's canvas, 3' wide
- *Other materials:* Paint, staples, string or wire, silicone caulk.

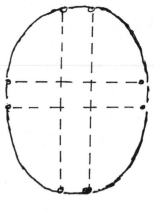

PLAN VIEW

trench drains
downhill

2' 2'

10" deep

LASHING
DETAIL

Framing

I. Begin by clearing an oblong-shaped area on the ground, 10′ wide by 12′ long. Measure and mark the pole locations. Dig a 6″ deep trench around the perimeter, to drain off water.

2. From the woods, find at least 28 slender, 1″–1½″ diameter saplings, as straight and long as possible, varying in length from 10′ to 6′. Ironwood, tamarack, maple, or any springy, pliable wood will do.

3. Use the longest, strongest poles for the entrance of the wigwam (poles #1 and #2). Sharpen the butt end of the poles and bury them in the ground at least 10″ deep and approximately 2′ apart. Then bury the two poles across from them (poles #3 and #4). Bury poles #5, #6, #7, and #8 in the same way, each 2′ apart. Install the 20 remaining poles, spaced 2′ apart. Make sure that all the poles lean slightly away from the center of the wigwam.

4. Beginning with poles #6 and #8, bend the tops downward and tie them together, using baling wire. Bend and tie together the tops of poles #5 and #7 in the same way. Continue tying opposite poles together along the long sides of the wigwam, making progressively lower arches toward the front and back of the structure.

5. Next, bend and tie the tops of the opposite poles on the short ends of the wigwam.

6. Lastly, bend and tie together pole #1 to pole #3 and pole #2 to pole #4. The highest point of the arch should be about 7½′.

7. Lash together each intersection of crosswise and lengthwise poles. First make loose, temporary lashings, make any necessary adjustments, and then tie the poles together firmly.

8. Make three horizontal frame pieces out of small saplings, using a pliable wood like poplar. It might be necessary to splice several thin saplings end to end to make poles long enough to go all the way around the wigwam.

9. Attach the first horizontal pole to the frame about 4″ above the ground. Begin at one side of the doorway and lash the pole to each arch until you reach the opposite side of the doorway.

10. Repeat with the top horizontal pole, which should be about 5′ from the ground. Then attach the middle horizontal pole about 2 feet from the top one.

Covering

Traditionally, Native Americans covered their wigwams with bark stripped from cedar or birch trees; however, since this will certainly kill the tree, we suggest substituting artist's canvas for bark.

1. Buy a 3′-wide roll of rough, primed artist's canvas and paint it with an off-white, oil-base paint. Brush the canvas with dark brown flecks of paint to make it look like birch bark.

2. Measure the bottom circumference of the wigwam and cut two strips of canvas to this length. Staple the first layer of canvas to the two lower horizontal poles, using a heavy-duty stapler and rust-resistant staples. Staple the second layer of canvas above the first layer, overlapping it by 6″.

3. Cut two thin strips of green wood, each one long enough to wrap around the canvas walls at the same height as the two lower horizontal poles.

4. Poke holes through the canvas, using a nail, and lash the inner and outer strips of wood together every 12″. (See Detail.) Seal the holes with clear silicone caulk.

5. Cut 6′-long canvas strips, place them across the top of the roof and secure them with string or wire lashed to the horizontal strips.

6. Leave a hole, 2′×2′, at the top of the wigwam for ventilation. When the weather is bad, cover the hole with a piece of canvas and hang a blanket over the entrance.

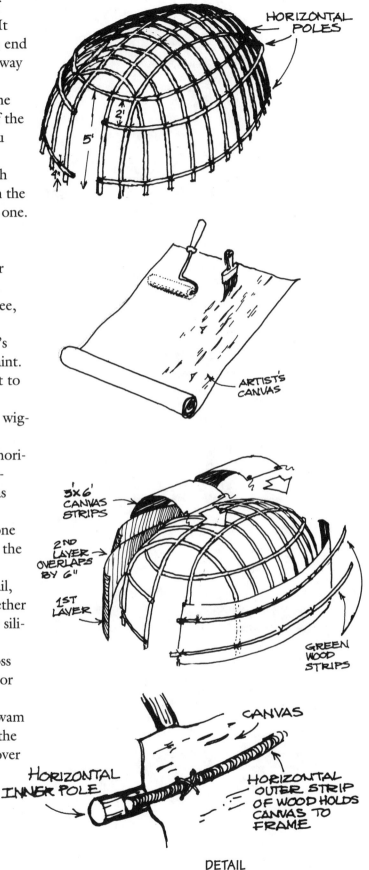

HORIZONTAL POLES

ARTIST'S CANVAS

3'×6' CANVAS STRIPS

2ND LAYER OVERLAPS BY 6″

1ST LAYER

GREEN WOOD STRIPS

HORIZONTAL INNER POLE

CANVAS

HORIZONTAL OUTER STRIP OF WOOD HOLDS CANVAS TO FRAME

DETAIL

Tipi

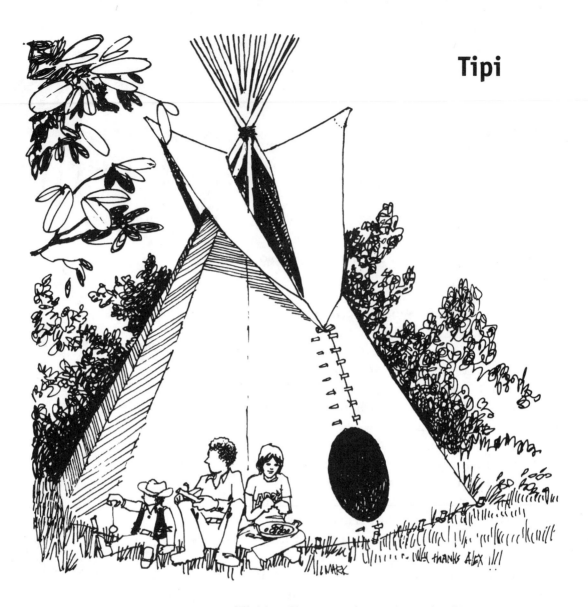

Materials Needed

- 15 straight poles, 25′ long and 3″– 4″ in diameter at the butt
- 2 lighter poles, 25′ long and 2″ in diameter at the butt
- 68 yards of 36″-wide canvas
- 11 dogwood lacing pins, 12″ long and ⅜″ in diameter
- 25 tent pegs, 18″ long
- ³⁄₁₆″ cord

Tipi is a Sioux word meaning "dwelling." Native Americans believed that there was no "power" in a square house and this may be one reason they lived in a shelter based on a circle. The design of the tipi is so perfect that it continues to be used today as a comfortable camping shelter, warm in the winter, cool in the summer, transportable, and easy to erect. It is picturesque and practical — a well-ventilated, all-weather tent, designed to withstand wind and driving rain. While "wigwam" refers to a woodland bark-covered shelter, the tipi is a plains type of shelter, conical in shape and covered with canvas. Spend one night in a tipi watching shadows on the wall and waking up with the first rays of early morning sun piercing through the smoke hole, and you will understand why the tipi inspires a kind of spiritual reverence.

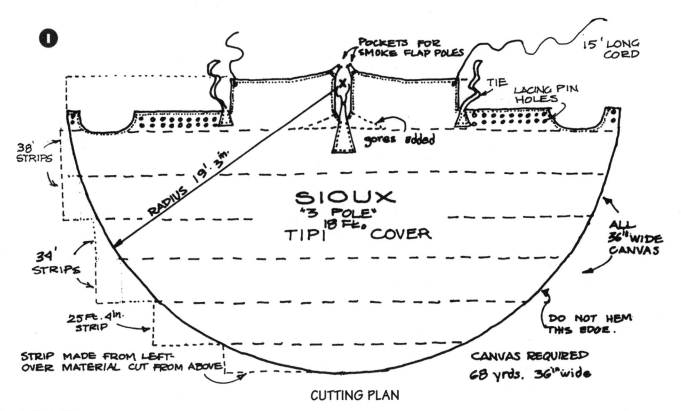

1

POCKETS FOR
SMOKE FLAP POLES

15' LONG
CORD

TIE

LACING PIN
HOLES

gores added

38'
STRIPS

RADIUS 19' 3 in.

SIOUX
"3 POLE"
18 FT.
TIPI COVER

34'
STRIPS

ALL
36" WIDE
CANVAS

25 FT. 4 in.
STRIP

DO NOT HEM
THIS EDGE.

STRIP MADE FROM LEFT-
OVER MATERIAL CUT FROM ABOVE!

CANVAS REQUIRED
68 yrds. 36" wide

CUTTING PLAN

Tipi Cover

The tipi cover, a semicircular shape with flaps at the opening, is stretched over a tilted conelike framework of poles. When erect, the back is steeper than the front. We have taken the dimensions of our tipi cover from an excellent book, *The Indian Tipi,* by Stanley Vestal. Unless you have an industrial sewing machine, we recommend giving the exact dimensions to a tent- or awning-maker and having him or her do the heavy sewing, instructing him to use flat seams. Choose a medium-weight canvas, 8–10 ounce duck, or any lightweight sturdy fabric. An emergency tipi cover can even be made out of parachute material. You can also buy ready-made tipi covers.

1. Cut strips of cloth to form a semicircle, laying them out like shingles, so water will run off the seams. (See Cutting Plan.)

2. Mark and cut the first strip as shown to make smoke flaps and lacing strips.

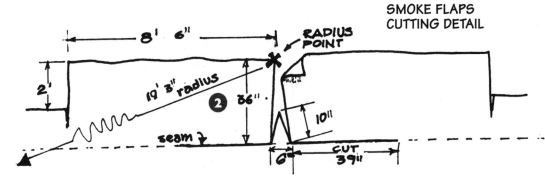

SMOKE FLAPS
CUTTING DETAIL

8' 6"

RADIUS
POINT

2'

19' 3" radius

2

36"

seam

10"

6"

CUT
39"

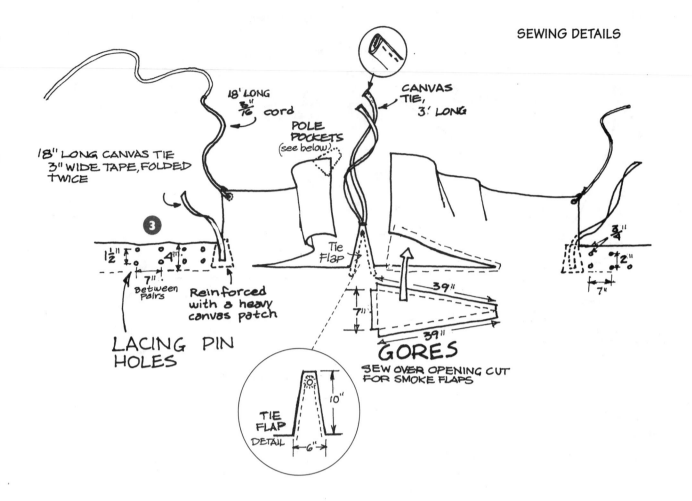

18' LONG $\frac{3}{16}$" cord

18" LONG CANVAS TIE 3" WIDE TAPE, FOLDED TWICE

CANVAS TIE, 3' LONG

POLE POCKETS (see below)

3

$1\frac{1}{2}$"

4"

7" Between Pairs

Reinforced with a heavy canvas patch

LACING PIN HOLES

Tie Flap

39"

7"

39"

GORES

SEW OVER OPENING CUT FOR SMOKE FLAPS

$\frac{3}{4}$"

2"

7"

TIE FLAP DETAIL

10"

6"

POLE POCKETS (Double-Thick Material)

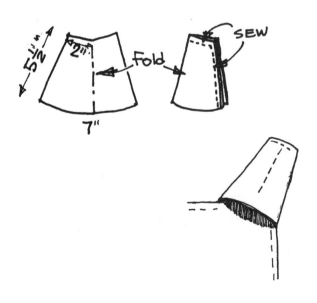

$5\frac{1}{2}$"

2"

Fold

SEW

7"

3. Mark and punch holes for smoke flap ties and lacing pins. Reinforce the edges of the holes with buttonhole stitches using beeswax thread.

4. Cut out reinforcement patches for the center tie flap and the two ties at the top of the lacing strips. Make ties from 3"-wide canvas folded over twice. Sew the reinforcement patches and the ties in place.

5. Cut gores as shown and sew them in place over the cuts made for the smoke flaps.

6. Make pole pockets from double-thick material. Turn the pockets inside out and sew them onto the corners of the smoke flaps.

Preparing the Poles

For an 18′ tipi, you will need 17 straight poles made from cedar, tamarack, or pine, each 25′ long. Poles should be 3″– 4″ at the butt and 2″ in diameter where they cross and tie. The two poles for the smoke flap should be smaller, measuring only 2″ thick at the butts. Select young trees, slightly larger than necessary, taking into consideration that without the bark and after the wood dries, the poles will be smaller.

1. Use a shaving buck made from two 6′ poles to support the tipi poles while you are peeling them. Remove even the tiniest burrs and protrusions from the poles to prevent water from accumulating and dripping on you.

2. Treat the butt ends of the poles with preservative. Then season the poles for three weeks, turning occasionally, to prevent them from later bowing under the weight of the cover.

Erecting the Poles

1. Choose and clear a site higher than the surrounding area and not directly under any trees. It should be near water and have access to plenty of firewood.

2. Select your three largest poles for the tripod. (Set aside the two lightest poles for the smoke flaps and a fourth heavy pole for the "lifting" pole.)

3. Lay two of the tripod poles side by side over the middle of the tipi cover with the butt ends protruding slightly past the bottom. Lay the third pole (which becomes the door pole) along the edge of the canvas, crossing the first two poles at a right angle. Mark each pole where it extends past the smoke flap.

4. Tie the poles together at the marks, using a clove-hitch knot. Make four turns around the poles and finish with two half-hitches. (See Plan View.)

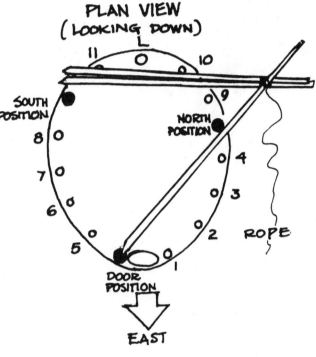

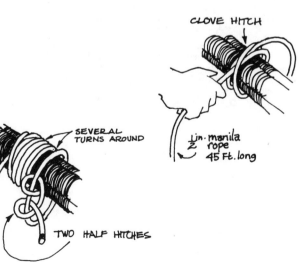

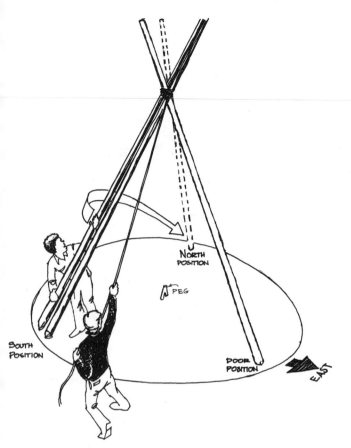

5. Have an assistant pull on the long end of the rope while you raise the poles, walking them up from underneath. To lock the tripod, spread one of the two side-by-side poles to the north position. This should lock the three poles in place.

6. Lay the remaining poles, using the sequence shown in the Plan View on page 115. Rest the first four poles in the front crotch, then place poles 5 and 8 on top of them. Place poles 9, 10, and 11 in the rear crotch. Note that only the first three poles are lashed together.

7. Walk the rope clockwise four times around the tripod, wrapping the rope tightly around the poles where they join. Then loop the rope around the pole in the north position and anchor it to a peg in the center.

Lifting the Cover

1. Fold the cover over once on each side, and then again, until you have a long triangular bundle. Tie the bundle to the lifting pole at point x.

2. Use the lifting pole to hoist the tipi cover into the remaining space in the rear of the tipi. Unfold the cover and walk it around to the front.

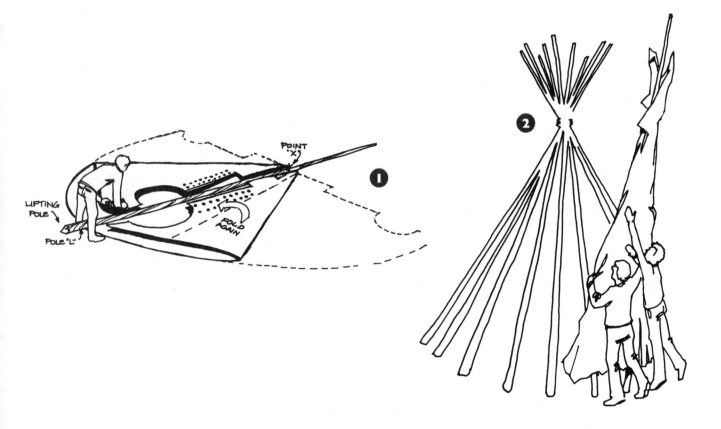

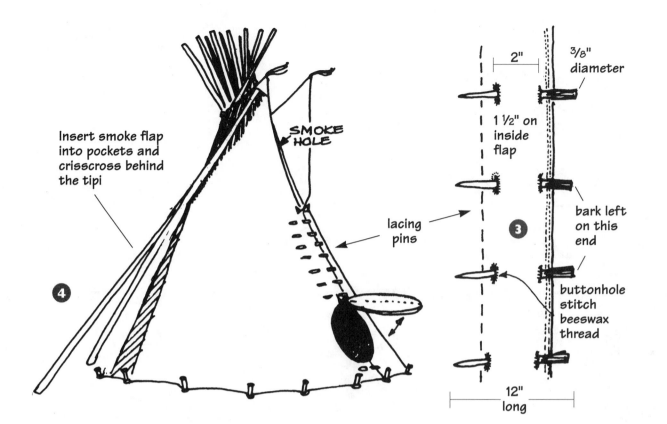

Insert smoke flap into pockets and crisscross behind the tipi

SMOKE HOLE

lacing pins

2"

3/8" diameter

1 1/2" on inside flap

bark left on this end

buttonhole stitch beeswax thread

12" long

3. Tie the cover together at the front, underneath the smoke flaps, and insert the lacing pins.

4. Insert smoke flap poles into pockets and crisscross the poles behind the tipi.

5. Make a cover for the door out of canvas sewn over a bentwood frame, or simply drape a blanket over the opening.

6. Tent pegs are secured to the tipi using a 3/16″-diameter rope tied to a pebble, pushed into the cloth from the inside of the tipi.

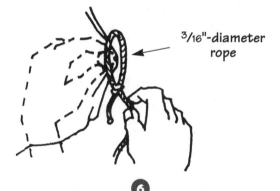

3/16″-diameter rope

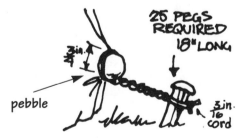

25 PEGS REQUIRED 18" LONG

3 in.

pebble

3 in. to cord

Yurt or "Ger"

The word "yurt," is a Turkish word that literally translates as "home." The yurt or "ger," as it is called in Mongolia, was used in the days of Marco Polo by Mongolian herdsmen, who needed a dwelling small and light enough to be moved easily and strong enough to withstand fierce wind and snow storms. When the grazing range of their animals became exhausted, the Mongolians would peel off the fur covering, fold up the lattice framing, and move to greener pastures. Gers are still commonplace in Mongolia, and their practical design has remained much the same. The front of the ger always faces southeast, away from the wind and toward the sacred sunrise. The yurt or ger is included here to give the reader a brief introduction to the subject. An excellent book, *Build a Yurt,* written by Len Charney, gives more detailed information about yurts.

Part	Quantity	Description
▶ *Platform*		
Foundation support	8	Concrete blocks
Frame	6	8′ 2x4
Floor	2	4′x8′ sheets of ¾″ exterior plywood
▶ *Wall frame*		
Lattice scissors	27	¾″x¼″ lattice strips, 36″ long
	27	⅜″x¼″ lattice strips, 37″ long
Cable	1	³⁄₁₆″-diameter cable, 28′ long
▶ *Roof*		
Roof members	54	1x2, 54″ long
Plywood rings	2	¾″ exterior plywood, approx. 24″ in diameter
Wall and roof cover		Approx. 40 yards heavy canvas in 36″-wide rolls
▶ *Door*		
Frame		Cut from one 10′ 1x4
Planking		1x6 tongue and groove
Other materials		Cable clamp, 6-mil polyethylene, waterproof sealant, 1″ copper nails, 3″ common nails, door hardware, old tire, 10′ post, ¼″ rope

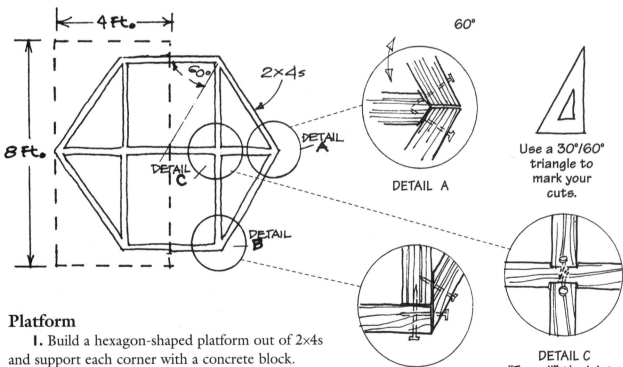

60°

Use a 30°/60° triangle to mark your cuts.

DETAIL A

DETAIL B

DETAIL C
"Toenail" the joints

Platform

1. Build a hexagon-shaped platform out of 2x4s and support each corner with a concrete block.

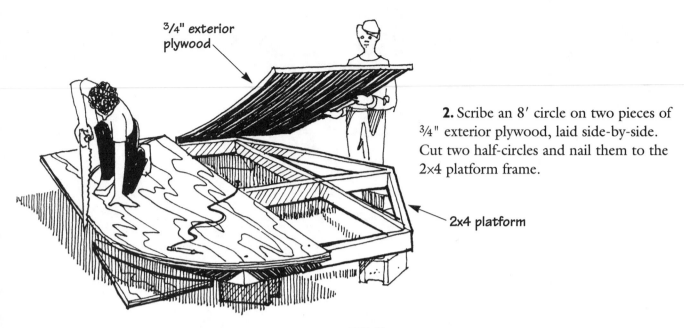

³⁄₄" exterior plywood

2. Scribe an 8′ circle on two pieces of ³⁄₄" exterior plywood, laid side-by-side. Cut two half-circles and nail them to the 2×4 platform frame.

2x4 platform

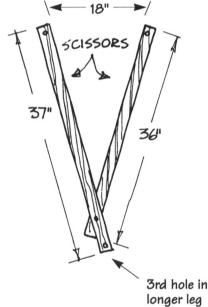

18"

SCISSORS

37"

36"

3rd hole in longer leg

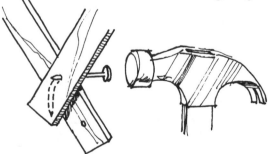

Each pair is nailed together and the nail is crimped over. Predrill holes to avoid splitting wood.

Wall

1. Make 27 pairs of "scissors" from 1⅜"×¼" lattice bought at your local lumber yard. Each pair of scissors has a 36" leg and a 37" leg. Put the two legs together so they are even at one end. Then drill holes through both pieces 1" from each end of the shorter leg. Insert a 1" copper nail through the hole at the end where the long leg extends beyond the short one. Crimp over the end of the nail to fasten the two legs together.

2. Drill a third hole in the longer leg of each pair of scissors, ½" from the end. This will prevent the lattice from splitting when it is nailed to the floor of the yurt.

3. Open all of the scissors so the two legs are 18" apart. Lay one of the scissors on the ground with the longer leg on top. Lay another scissors next to the first, 12" to the right, so the longer leg of the second scissors rests on top of the lower leg of the first. Continue laying out the rest of the scissors, each 12" to the right of the one before. You will find that the ends of the legs start lining up at 6" intervals.

4. Mark off 6" increments along a 28′ length of ³⁄₁₆"-diameter cable.

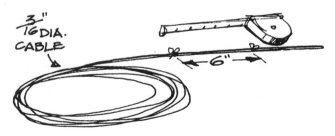

3⁄16" DIA. CABLE

6"

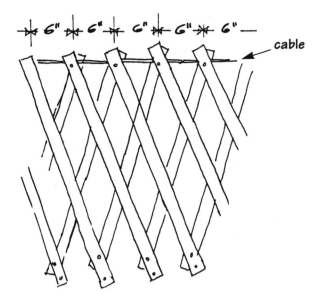

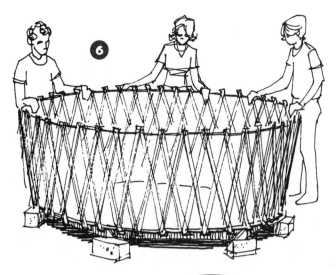

5. Lay the cable on top of the row of scissors and sandwich it between the ends of two overlapping legs at each 6″ mark. Fasten the legs together with a nail inserted through the pre-drilled holes. Crimp the nail to squeeze the cable between the legs. Notice that the nail goes *under* the cable. Continue along the lattice until all of the overlapping legs have been connected.

6. With help from friends, shape the completed lattice to form a circle around the floor of the yurt. Draw the wire tight and secure it with a clamp. The legs of the scissors at either end of the lattice should now line up so they can be fastened with nails inserted through the pre-drilled holes.

7. Nail the longer outside leg of each pair of lattice scissors to the edge of the plywood floor. Use 2″ common nails inserted through the pre-drilled holes.

8. Cut out a door opening.

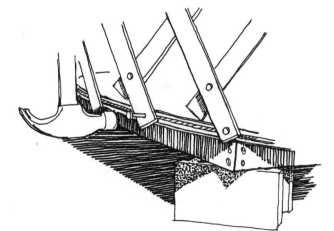

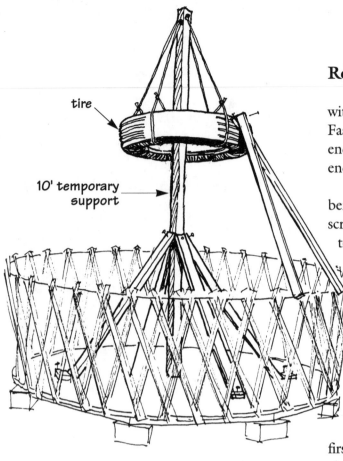

tire

10' temporary support

Roof

1. Make 27 pairs of roof members. Assemble with the bottom leg flat and the top leg on edge. Fasten the two pieces together with a nail at one end. Drill a hole through both legs 1″ from the other end. Then open the legs so they are 12″ apart.

2. Make a temporary support for the roof members, using an old automobile tire, a 10′ post, and scrap lumber as shown. Suspend the tire from the top of the post so it hangs about 6 feet above the floor.

3. Put the first roof member in place with the legs resting on the cable at the top of the lattice wall and the top resting against the tire.

4. Put the second roof member in place with its top leg overlapping the bottom leg of the first one. Put those two legs together with the cable clamped between them. Secure the legs by inserting a nail through the pre-drilled holes and bending it over. Make sure that the nail is behind the cable as viewed from outside the yurt.

5. Add the rest of the roof members, attaching the overlapping legs with the cable between them, until the entire frame of the roof is in place. Then remove the temporary support by lowering the tire to the ground. The roof members will come together to form a tight ring.

6. Make a ring of ¾″ exterior plywood to fit over the hole in the roof and nail it to the roof members. This will serve as the base for the skylight.

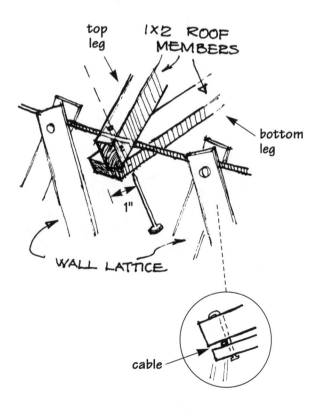

top leg

1X2 ROOF MEMBERS

bottom leg

1″

WALL LATTICE

cable

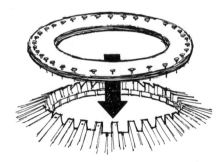

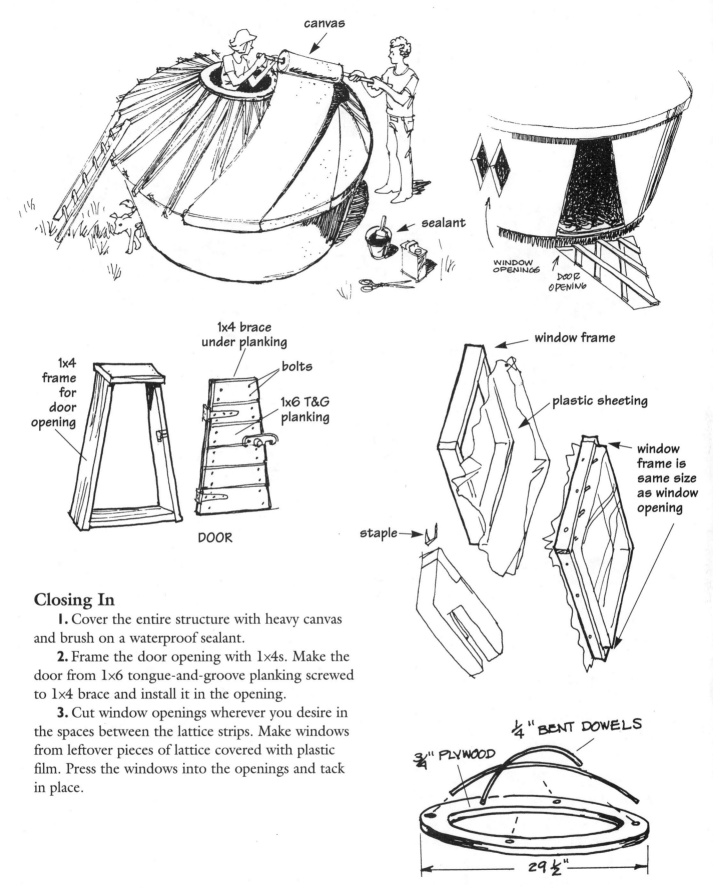

canvas

sealant

WINDOW OPENINGS

DOOR OPENING

1x4 frame for door opening

1x4 brace under planking

bolts

1x6 T&G planking

DOOR

window frame

plastic sheeting

window frame is same size as window opening

staple

Closing In

1. Cover the entire structure with heavy canvas and brush on a waterproof sealant.

2. Frame the door opening with 1x4s. Make the door from 1x6 tongue-and-groove planking screwed to 1x4 brace and install it in the opening.

3. Cut window openings wherever you desire in the spaces between the lattice strips. Make windows from leftover pieces of lattice covered with plastic film. Press the windows into the openings and tack in place.

¼" BENT DOWELS

¾" PLYWOOD

29 ½"

SKYLIGHT

Stacked-Log Hogan

Materials Needed

- **Walls:** 54 logs, 8"–10" in diameter and 10' long
- **Roof:** 40 logs, 4"–8" in diameter, 4'–8' long
- **Chinking:** Small branches, bark, wet earth
- **Door frame:** Cut to fit from two pieces of 2×9, 10' long
- **Door paneling:** Cut to fit from six pieces of rough 1×10 cedar, 8' long
- **Door battens:** Two pieces of 1×6, approx. 26" long
- **Hatch frame:** Four pieces of 2×9, approx. 30" long
- **Hatch cover:** Four pieces of 1×4, approx. 30" long
- **Other materials:** 6"–10" spikes, canvas

This hexagonal hogan originated in the southwest part of the United States and was a typical dwelling for the Navajo Indians. The word "hogan" means "home place" in the Navajo language, and the door always faces east, toward the rising sun. The Navajo consider hogans "alive," and house-blessing songs are sung to ensure harmony, beauty, and protection for the occupants. Walls of the hogan are layered in a sequence of interlocking poles, chinked with cedar bark, packed with wet earth, and topped with a corbelled log roof.

Foundation

1. Begin by marking a 16'-diameter circle on the ground.

2. Using a radius of 8', scribe six arcs around the circle, marking six equidistant points to make the corners of the hexagon.

3. Mound up the dirt inside the circle so rain water won't seep into the hogan after it is finished.

Walls

1. Cut 54 peeled logs, 8"–10" in diameter and 10' long, for the walls.

2. Using a chain saw, notch all the logs halfway through to form a saddle joint 12" from each end. This joint is similar to a "log cabin" joint, except the notches are cut at a 60° angle across the log instead of straight across, so the stacked logs will form a hexagon.

3. Use the thickest logs for the bottom course and fill the gap under the logs with rocks and soil.

4. Build up nine courses of logs (see "Log Cabin," page 130).

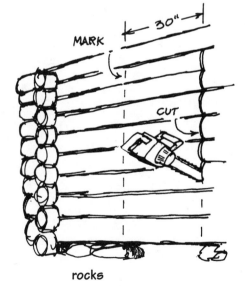

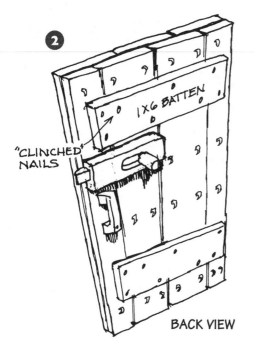

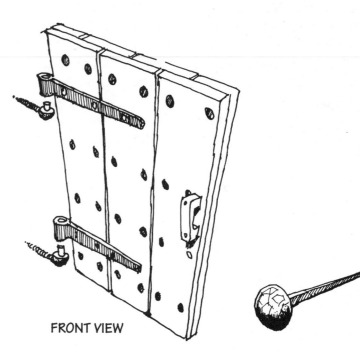

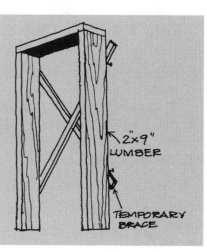

BACK VIEW   FRONT VIEW

Door

1. Mark and cut a 30″ wide door opening in the wall. Do not cut through the top log. Frame the doorway with rough 2×9 lumber (sold as scaffolding at lumber yards).

2. Make the door from six pieces of 1×10 rough cedar boards. Rip one board in half lengthwise for the back side of the door. Nail the boards together, staggering the joints and clinching the nails over on the back side.

▶ TIP

Make the door frame first and use it as a template to mark the door opening. Attach a temporary brace to keep it square until it is installed. Nail the door frame to the ends of the logs once the frame is in place.

Roof

1. The roof is made of unnotched logs, stacked concentrically in increasingly smaller hexagons until a dome is formed. Cut approximately 40 logs, 4″–8″ in diameter, varying in length from 4′–8′. As you build the roof, stack each log so the ends rest on two logs below it and nail down the ends using 6″–10″ spikes.

2. Fill any spaces with smaller logs or branches and cover the roof with bark and wet earth.

3. Leave a 30″ square hole at the top of the roof and frame it with 2x9 boards. Cover the top with canvas, attached with flat-head roofing nails.

4. Make a hatch for the roof opening using 1x4 lumber. Use a forked stick to prop the hatch open.

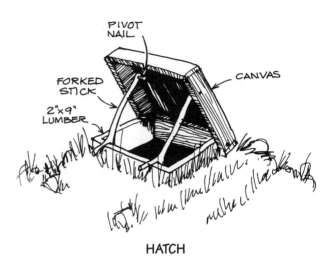

HATCH

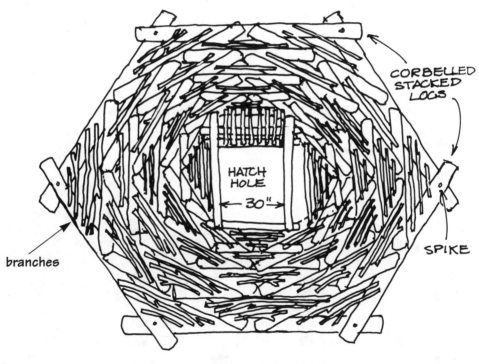

ROOF — PLAN VIEW

CHAPTER 8

Little Houses

There is some of the same fitness in a man's building his own house
that here is in a bird's building its own nest. . . .
Shall we forever resign the pleasure of construction to the carpenter?

Henry David Thoreau, *Walden*

The idea of building a house is daunting enough to intimidate most amateur carpenters. But if you have mastered the skills required to build the other shelters in this book, there is no reason to think that a small house would be too much for you. Building a house is really just a matter of completing a series of small projects, any of which would seem quite manageable on their own. It's not a question of whether you have the ability to do it, but whether you have the interest, time, and energy.

Each of the three small houses in this section is built with techniques used in other projects that we have already covered. Even the Writer's Retreat (shown right and on pages 136 to 140), which is perhaps the least "rustic" in appearance of all the houses, is fairly simple in structure. We'll guide you through the major steps, but many of the details will be left up to you. Our plans are just the starting point. It's your ideas, as well as your labor, that will make the house your own.

WRITER'S RETREAT INTERIOR

Log Cabin

If you are anxious to escape from the pressures that accompany today's fast pace of living, and you are able to devote yourself to a substantial, long-term project, then this log cabin is for you.

Three essentials before you begin building are: some property with a beautiful view, a large supply of straight logs, and a passion for working with wood, since building a log cabin is definitely a labor of love.

The following materials list gives the approximate number of logs necessary for a 9′×12′ cabin. The exact number of logs you will need depends on the dimensions of your particular cabin. It is always a good idea to have extra logs, since some may end up having too many knots or not being straight enough. A 9′×12′ cabin, although small, is an adequate size and more heat-efficient than a larger cabin. With each person giving off as much heat as a 100 watt bulb, it is fairly easy to warm up this amont of space. Everything in this cabin is hand-built, with the exception of the fireplace. We recommend you buy a zero-clearance, factory-made steel liner and build a stone fireplace around it.

Part	Quantity	Description
Front and back sills	2	9" diameter, 14' long
Girder	1	7" diameter, 12' long
Side sills	2	9" diameter, 14' long
Front and back logs	20	7" diameter, 14' long
	2	8" diameter, 15' long
Side logs	20	7" diameter, 11' long
	2	8" diameter, 13' long
Gable logs	8	7" diameter, from 2' to 10' long
Ridge pole and purlins	3	8" diameter, 15' long
Rafters	8	4" diameter, 8' long

If you are unable to find enough logs near your cabin site, it may be necessary to have a sawmill cut them and deliver them to you. Or, if you know someone with a large stand of good, straight trees, you may be able to selectively cull out trees that are growing too close together. Use the handcart shown on page 7 to help you carry the trees from the woods to the road. From this point you can haul the logs to your building site using a trailer or truck. If your cabin site is on a lake or river, consider rafting the logs over, or even carrying them by canoe.

1000 LBS. OF LOGS

White pine, black pine, fir, white spruce, and balsam — in short, most coniferous or evergreen trees — make excellent poles for building log cabins. The best time to cut the logs is in the spring, while the sap is running.

Preparing Logs

1. Peeling the bark off the logs removes hiding places for insects and prevents decay. Most conifers can be peeled easily by making two cuts down the length of the log, about 1½" apart. Use a large screwdriver to pry up the bark between the cuts at one end. Grab the bark and pull it down to the other end.

2. Turn the log slightly and make another cut lengthwise, continuing until the entire log is peeled. Peeling goes quite quickly and should only take 10–15 minutes per log.

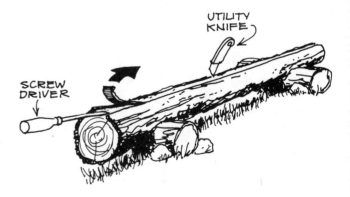

UTILITY KNIFE

SCREW DRIVER

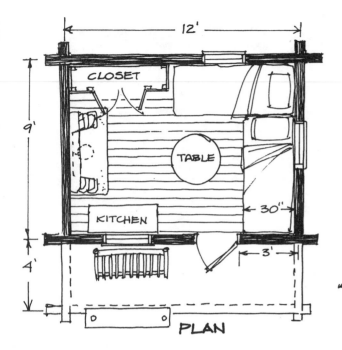

CLOSET

TABLE

KITCHEN

30"

3'

12'

9'

4'

PLAN

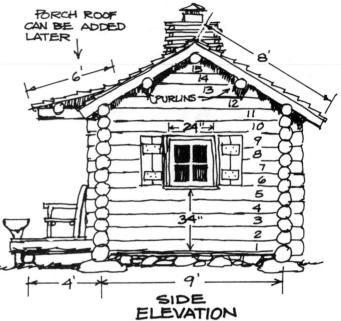

PORCH ROOF CAN BE ADDED LATER

PURLINS

6'

8'

15

14

13

12

11

10

9

8

7

6

5

4

3

2

1

24"

34"

4'

9'

SIDE ELEVATION

Foundation

1. Mark the "foot print" of your cabin on the ground and hammer pegs in the ground at the points where your footings will go.

2. Use a pick ax and shovel to level the ground and place a large flat rock at each of the 12 footing points. Check to make sure that the tops of the rocks are at the same level.

3. Fill the space below the beams with rocks and dirt to prevent skunks, opossums, chipmunks, and other creatures from making your home their home.

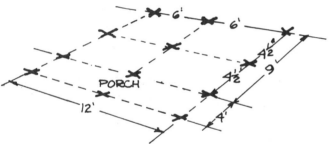

6'

6'

4½'

4½'

9'

4'

PORCH

12'

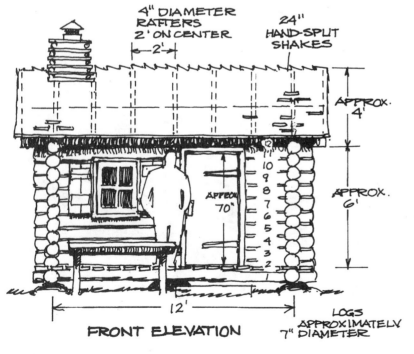

4" DIAMETER RAFTERS 2' ON CENTER

2'

24" HAND-SPLIT SHAKES

APPROX. 4'

APPROX. 6'

APPROX. 70"

12

11

10

9

8

7

6

5

4

3

2

1

12'

FRONT ELEVATION

LOGS APPROXIMATELY 7" DIAMETER

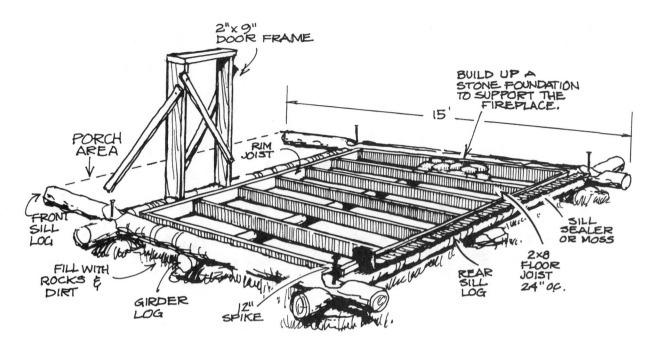

4. Lay down the front and rear sill logs first, using the thickest ones available, then notch and lay down the two longer side logs. Measure the diagonals to make sure the foundation logs are square and drive a 12″ spike into each corner.

5. Use your straightest log for the girder, which is placed midway between the front and rear logs.

Floor

1. Cut two 2×8 rim joists, 12′ long, to fit inside the front and rear logs and nail them in place.

2. Cut seven 2×8 floor joists to fit between the rim joists. Toe-nail the joists to the inside of the frame, spacing them 24″ on center.

3. Adjust the height of the girder by placing stones under it to raise it or digging out a trench underneath to lower it. Once the girder touches the bottoms of all the floor joists, nail it to the side beams.

4. Cut and nail 2×6 tongue-and-groove barn flooring over the entire floor frame.

Walls

1. Before adding the second layer of logs to the walls, build a frame for the door out of 2×9 scaffolding and nail it temporarily in place. Build the wall around the door frame, driving spikes through the frame into the log ends as you go.

2. As you proceed building up the walls, alternate the butt ends and the smaller ends so the logs

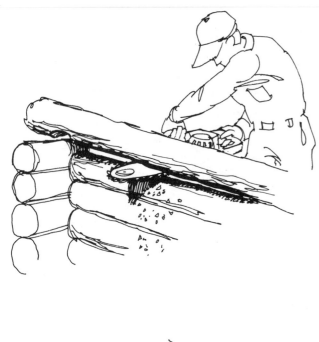

remain level. Check to make sure the *inside* walls are plumb. Lay a strip of fiberglass sill sealer or moss between each layer of logs to avoid any gaps later on.

3. If you find that some of your logs don't lie together perfectly, run a chain saw between them to smooth off the rough edges or bumps.

4. Log #12 on the front and rear walls extends 1½' past the sides of the cabin to support the roof rafters.

5. Continue building up the two side (gable) walls, stopping after log #13 to add two 15' logs (purlins) to the front and back.

6. Finish the top with another 15' log (the ridge pole).

Roof

1. Cut eighteen 4"-diameter rafter poles, each 8' long, and nail them to the purlins and ridge pole every 2'.

2. Cover them with 1×6 eastern pine and hand-split cedar shakes (see "Roofs," page 17). The roof pitch or slant should be steep enough to allow the rain to run off quickly, yet flat enough to walk on without slipping.

Chinking

As mentioned earlier, the logs are caulked with fiberglass or moss insulation during construction. After the cabin is finished, the logs will continue to dry out, leaving spaces that need to be chinked. Use premixed mortar to fill the gaps and spaces between logs. To help hold the chinking in place, hammer nails every 6" along each log before applying the mortar.

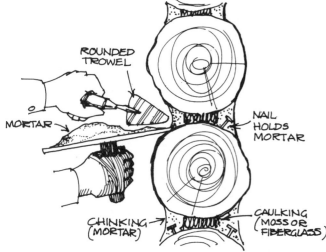

Handmade Windows

1. Mark and cut window openings in the log walls.

2. Insert the 2×8 window frames into the walls and nail them to the log ends.

3. Make windows out of two thicknesses of ¾" cedar, lapped and glued at the corners. Use ⅛"-thick tempered glass and seal with ¾"×¾" strips of wood beveled at 45°. The removable windows are held in the frame by a ¾"×¾" stop at the bottom and a spring-loaded catch at the top. When open, they tilt in and are supported by a string tied to an eye screw at the top of the window frame.

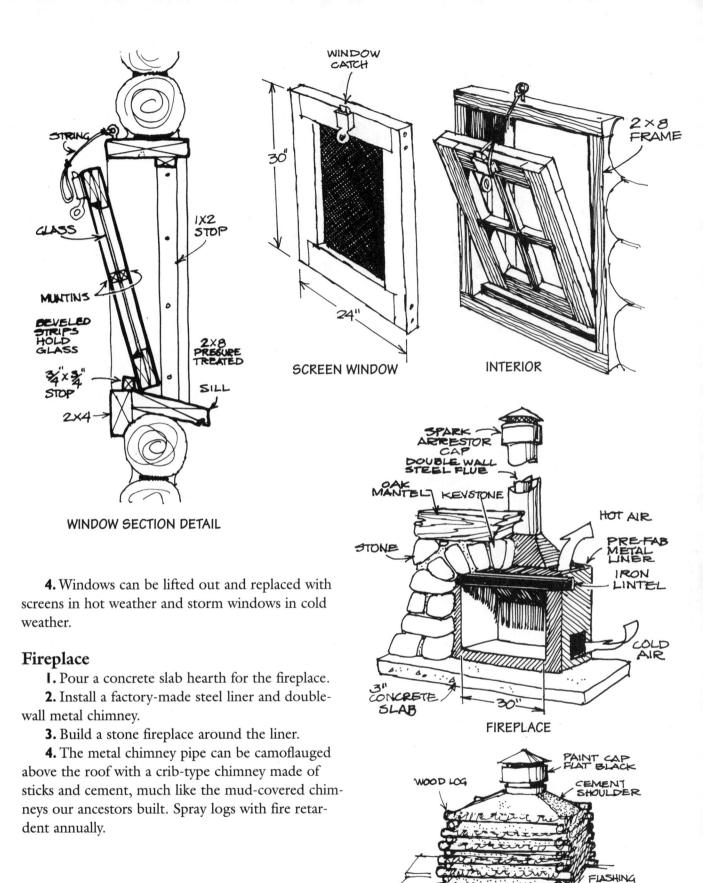

STRING

GLASS

MUNTINS

BEVELED STRIPS HOLD GLASS

3/4" X 3/4" STOP

2X4

1X2 STOP

2X8 PRESSURE TREATED

SILL

WINDOW SECTION DETAIL

WINDOW CATCH

30"

24"

SCREEN WINDOW

2X8 FRAME

INTERIOR

SPARK ARRESTOR CAP

DOUBLE WALL STEEL FLUE

OAK MANTEL

KEYSTONE

STONE

HOT AIR

PRE-FAB METAL LINER

IRON LINTEL

COLD AIR

3" CONCRETE SLAB

30"

FIREPLACE

PAINT CAP FLAT BLACK

WOOD LOG

CEMENT SHOULDER

FLASHING

MUD

CHIMNEY

4. Windows can be lifted out and replaced with screens in hot weather and storm windows in cold weather.

Fireplace

1. Pour a concrete slab hearth for the fireplace.

2. Install a factory-made steel liner and double-wall metal chimney.

3. Build a stone fireplace around the liner.

4. The metal chimney pipe can be camoflauged above the roof with a crib-type chimney made of sticks and cement, much like the mud-covered chimneys our ancestors built. Spray logs with fire retardent annually.

Writer's Retreat

Today, more people than ever are working out of their homes. The advantages are numerous; the disadvantage, of course, being that it's hard to maintain your privacy and concentration. This writer's retreat can be built close to home but still gives you a space of your own. With windows on two sides, it's designed for a spot with a view of the horizon, the sea, or open sky to help keep a clear mind. This is a space that you can design and fill with the essentials that express your way of life. The entire structure is well insulated and requires only a couple of electric heaters to keep it toasty warm.

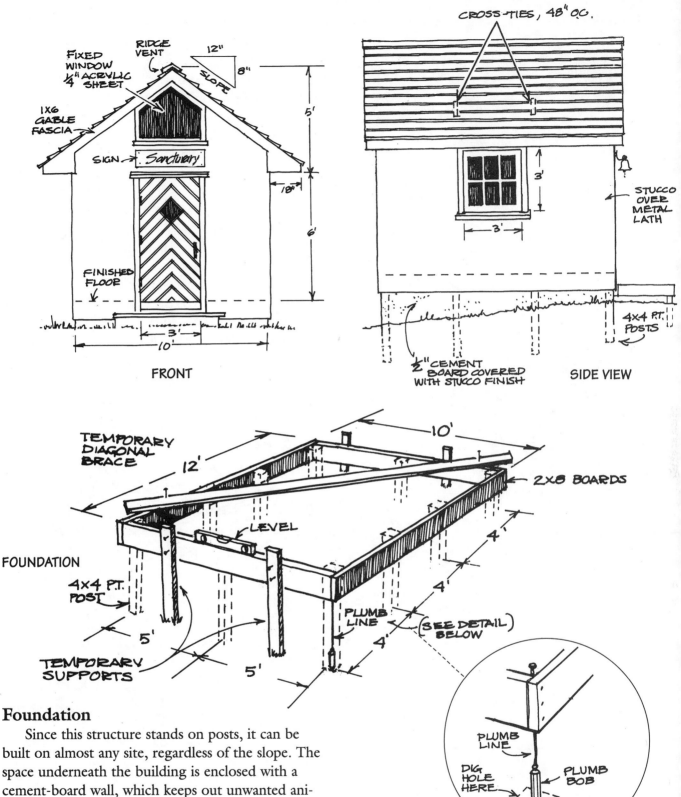

FIXED WINDOW ¼" ACRYLIC SHEET

RIDGE VENT

1X6 GABLE FASCIA

12"

SLOPE

8"

5'

SIGN — Sanctuary

18"

6'

FINISHED FLOOR

3'

10'

FRONT

CROSS-TIES, 48" O.C.

3'

3'

STUCCO OVER METAL LATH

4X4 P.T. POSTS

2" CEMENT BOARD COVERED WITH STUCCO FINISH

SIDE VIEW

TEMPORARY DIAGONAL BRACE

12'

10'

LEVEL

2X8 BOARDS

FOUNDATION

4X4 P.T. POST

5'

TEMPORARY SUPPORTS

5'

4'

4'

PLUMB LINE

(SEE DETAIL BELOW)

4'

PLUMB LINE

DIG HOLE HERE

PLUMB BOB

MARK

Foundation

Since this structure stands on posts, it can be built on almost any site, regardless of the slope. The space underneath the building is enclosed with a cement-board wall, which keeps out unwanted animals and provides a way to insulate under the floor.

1. The easiest way to construct the foundation is to nail together four 2x8 boards to form a 12'×10' frame. After checking to make sure the diagonals are equal, temporarily nail a piece of scrap wood diagonally across the frame to keep it square.

2. Use the frame as a guide to mark where the post holes will go. Level the floor frame, drop a plumb line down the inside of one corner, and make a mark on the ground where the outside corner of the post will go. Use the same procedure to mark where the other posts will go.

3. Move the frame aside and dig ten 6″-diameter holes, 30″ deep, at the marks. Place the frame back in position.

4. After leveling the frame, hold it in place at each end with two temporary supports. Cut and insert a 4×4 pressure-treated post in each hole and nail the frame to the posts.

5. Dig a 6″-deep trench around the posts and nail ½″-thick cement board to the outside of the posts below the frame. Cover the outside of the cement board with pre-mixed bonding cement. Backfill the trench.

FLOOR FRAME

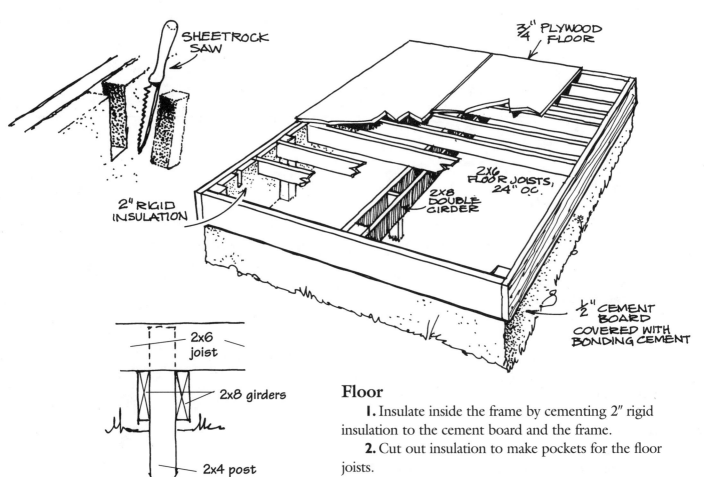

SHEETROCK SAW

2″ RIGID INSULATION

¾″ PLYWOOD FLOOR

2×6 FLOOR JOISTS, 24″ O.C.

2×8 DOUBLE GIRDER

½″ CEMENT BOARD COVERED WITH BONDING CEMENT

2×6 joist

2×8 girders

2×4 post

Floor

1. Insulate inside the frame by cementing 2″ rigid insulation to the cement board and the frame.

2. Cut out insulation to make pockets for the floor joists.

3. Build a girder to support the floor joists out of two pieces of 2×6 with 2×4 posts wedged between them.

4. Nail the 2×4 floor joists to the floor frame, spaced 24″ on center.

5. Cover the joists with a ¾″ exterior-plywood floor.

Framing

1. Frame the walls with 2×6 sole and top plates and 2×6 studs. Build each wall flat on the floor and tilt it up into position, then nail the walls together at the corners.

2. Use doubled 2×6s with 2×3 spacers for headers over the windows and doors.

3. Frame the roof with 2×8 rafters meeting at a 1×6 ridge board.

4. Attach two 2×6 crossties, 4′ on center, across two pairs of rafters to keep the walls from spreading.

Roof

We recommend covering the roof with 18″ cedar shingles, which are "woodsy" looking but less rustic than hand-split shakes.

1. Nail the ceiling (sheetrock or shiplapped pine) to the underside of the rafters inside the house.

2. Lay a double layer of 2½″ extruded polystyrene (blueboard) on top of the ceiling between the rafters.

3. Cut 1×6 fascia boards to fit the angle of the roof and nail them to the rafter ends.

4. Nail 1×4 spaced sheathing on top of the rafters and install a ridge vent at the peak of the roof.

5. Nail ⅜″-plywood soffits under the rafters where they extend over the walls. Provide vents in the soffits to allow air to circulate under the roof.

6. Nail cedar shingles onto the spaced sheathing, giving each row a 5½″ exposure to the weather.

Exterior Walls

Stuccoing the cabin results in a finished surface that never has to be painted and is practically maintenance free.

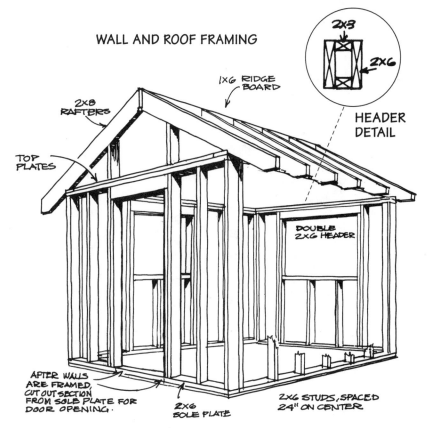

WALL AND ROOF FRAMING

HEADER DETAIL

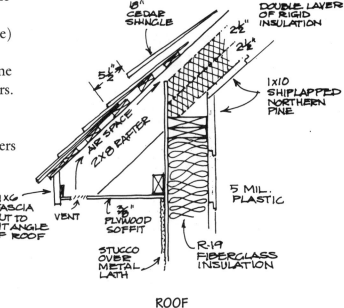

ROOF

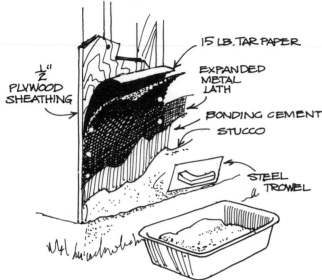

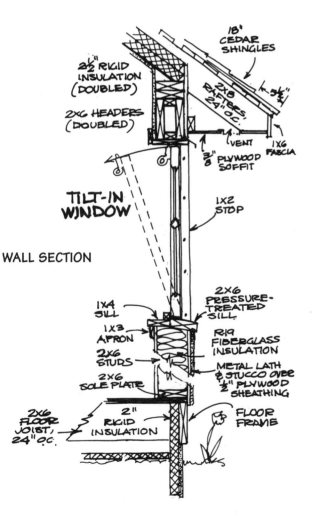

1. Sheath the exterior walls with ½″ exterior plywood.

2. Staple 15 lb. tar paper to the plywood sheathing. Staple metal lath over the tar paper, using ⅞″ staples.

3. Cover the walls with an acrylic bonding cement (sold in masonry yards). This results in a strong, elastic finish (sometimes called "structural skin"). Although it can be used alone, it is more attractive to cover this with stucco, which is sold in bags. After scratching the first coat, use a trowel to apply a ¼″-thick coat of stucco.

Interior Walls

1. Insulate the walls with R-19 fiberglass batts between the studs.

2. Staple 5-mil plastic sheeting to the studs and cover it with sheetrock or shiplapped pine.

Finish the house with windows, doors, and details of your choice. After you have hammered in the last nail, enjoy the silence of the enclosed space you have created — a space for contemplation or activity — in any case, a space of your own.

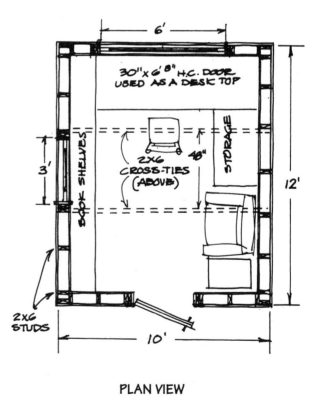

PLAN VIEW

David Hense's Little House

This little house epitomizes the philosophy of this book, which is to inspire the reader to build one of the book's designs, modifying it if necessary to fit his or her needs. Using the foot print of the 8′×10′ Garden Cordwood Hut (see page 36) as inspiration, David Hense modified the design and construction to suit his personal taste, substituting cedar shingles over 2×3 studs for the cemented log ends and adding on a small potting shed for his wife.

Because he lives in the Northwest, where temperatures can plunge dramatically, David insulated the shed and finished the inside using tongue-and-groove hemlock boards. Recycled windows were scraped down, painted, and reglazed. A potbelly stove provides warmth and is especially useful when power is lost due to a winter storm. It takes only minutes for the little house to reach a comfortable temperature, even on the coldest days.

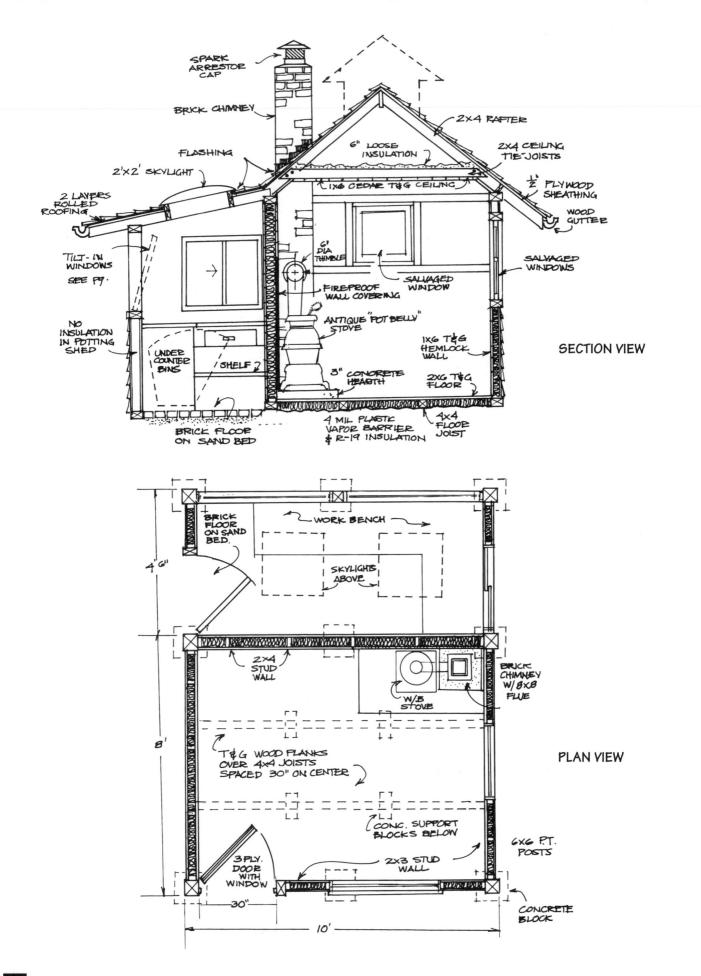

SPARK
ARRESTOR
CAP

BRICK CHIMNEY

FLASHING

2'x2' SKYLIGHT

2 LAYERS
ROLLED
ROOFING

TILT-IN
WINDOWS
SEE P9.

NO
INSULATION
IN POTTING
SHED

UNDER
COUNTER
BINS

SHELF

BRICK FLOOR
ON SAND BED

6" LOOSE
INSULATION

1X6 CEDAR T&G CEILING

6" DIA
THIMBLE

FIREPROOF
WALL COVERING

ANTIQUE "POT BELLY"
STOVE

3" CONCRETE
HEARTH

4 MIL PLASTIC
VAPOR BARRIER
& R-19 INSULATION

2x4 RAFTER

2x4 CEILING
TIE JOISTS

½" PLYWOOD
SHEATHING

WOOD
GUTTER

SALVAGED
WINDOW

SALVAGED
WINDOWS

1X6 T&G
HEMLOCK
WALL

2x6 T&G
FLOOR

4x4
FLOOR
JOIST

SECTION VIEW

BRICK
FLOOR
ON SAND
BED.

4' 6"

2x4
STUD
WALL

T&G WOOD PLANKS
OVER 4x4 JOISTS
SPACED 30" ON CENTER

8'

3 PLY.
DOOR
WITH
WINDOW

30"

WORK BENCH

SKYLIGHTS
ABOVE

W/B
STOVE

BRICK
CHIMNEY
W/ 8X8
FLUE

CONC. SUPPORT
BLOCKS BELOW

6x6 P.T.
POSTS

2x3 STUD
WALL

CONCRETE
BLOCK

PLAN VIEW

10'

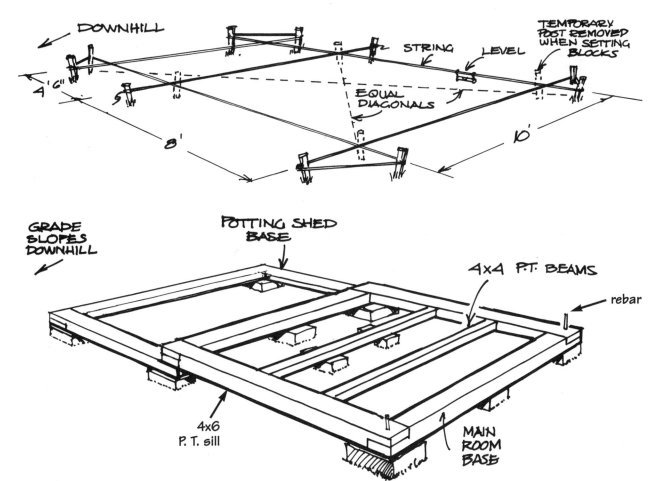

Foundation

1. Begin by laying out the foot print of the structure by driving in temporary posts at the corners. Check to make sure that the diagonals are equal, and extend strings 3′ past each corner and around a short post, as shown. This allows you to remove the string when you are setting the blocks and replace it later to make sure that the building is lined up correctly.

2. Use a mason's line to make the strings level at a height 4″ above the highest ground. Place concrete blocks at the corners to meet the level of the string. Note: The potting shed is stepped down from the main room to allow a greater pitch for the roof.

3. Cut and lay 4×6 pressure-treated sills on the concrete blocks, making lap joints where they meet.

4. Add two 4×4 pressure-treated beams to support the floor of the main room.

5. Fill the potting shed base with sand in preparation for the brick floor.

6. Drill a hole in each corner of the sills and insert a ½″-diameter piece of rebar, allowing 4″ of rebar to protrude.

CHIMNEY-BLOCK PIER

> ▶ **TIP**

Chimney blocks, sold at masonry supply yards, make excellent piers. Simply set in place and fill the core with concrete.

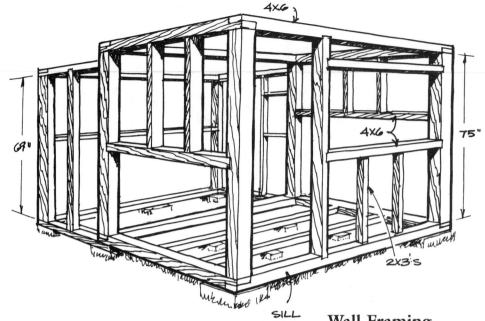

SILL

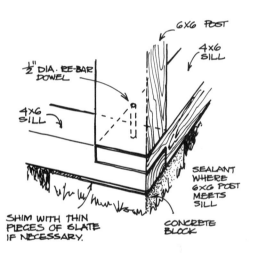

6×6 POST

4×6 SILL

½" DIA. RE-BAR DOWEL

4×6 SILL

SEALANT WHERE 6×6 POST MEETS SILL

SHIM WITH THIN PIECES OF SLATE IF NECESSARY.

CONCRETE BLOCK

CORNER DETAIL

Wall Framing

1. Frame the walls with 6×6 posts and 4×6 beams. Drill ½"-diameter holes in the ends of the corner posts to fit over the rebar inserted into the sills. (For more details on framing, see the Garden Cordwood Hut on page 36.)

2. Frame the door and window openings with 2×6 lumber.

3. After the heavy framing is finished, fill in the exterior walls with 2×3 studs spaced 24" on center.

4. Frame the wall between the main room and the potting shed with 2×4 studs spaced 24" on center.

Roof Framing

1. Frame the roof with 2×4 rafters spaced 24" on center. The rafters over the main room meet at a 1×6 ridge beam and are tied together with 2×4 joists.

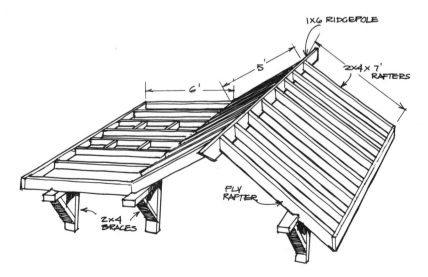

1×6 RIDGEPOLE

2×4 × 7' RAFTERS

5'

6'

FLY RAFTER

2×4 BRACES

2. Make 2×4 braces and nail them to the corner posts to support the fly rafters.

3. Insert 2×4 headers between the rafters over the potting shed to frame the two skylights.

4. Cover the ends of the rafters with 1×4 fascia boards.

Sheathing

1. Cover the exterior walls with ½″ plywood nailed to the studs. Also sheath the wall between the main room and the potting shed, leaving the studs exposed in the main room.

2. Cover the plywood on the lower part of the walls (up to the eaves) with 18″ cedar shingles.

3. On the gable ends, cover the top part of the walls with 1×6 cedar boards and 1×2 cedar battens. Provide a louvered vent on each of the gable ends.

4. Nail 1×6 boards to the underside of the ceiling joists over the main room. Pour a 6″ layer of loose insulation on top of the ceiling boards, then sheath the roof over the main room and the potting shed with ½″ plywood.

Floor

1. Spread overlapping sheets of 4-mil plastic under the floor joists in the main room.

2. To help support the ends of the floor boards, nail 2×4 ledger boards to the inside of the sills.

3. Nail 2×6 tongue-and-groove planks to the floor joists.

4. Lay a level brick floor on top of 4″ of sand to make the floor for the potting shed.

Interior Walls

1. Insulate the walls of the main room with R-19 fiberglass wool. (The potting shed is not insulated.)

2. Cover the insulation with 1×6 tongue-and-groove hemlock, except near the stove, where the walls should be covered with a noncombustible material such as slate, tile, or cement board.

Chimney and Hearth

1. Cast a 3″-thick concrete hearth.

2. Build a brick chimney, two bricks wide, lined with an 8″ clay flue. Extend the chimney 2½′ above the roof and finish it off with a cement collar and a metal spark arrestor.

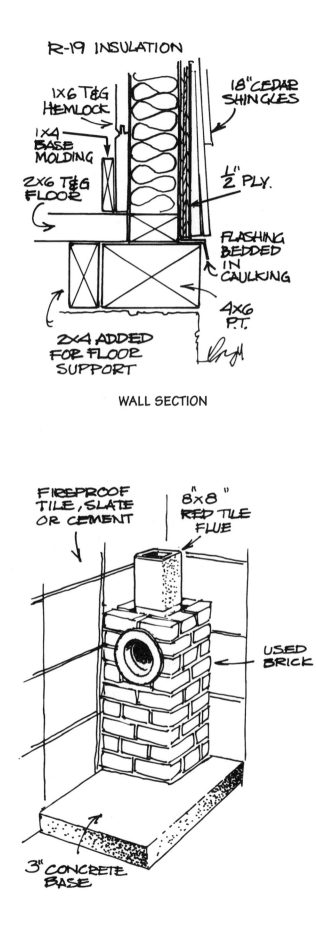

R-19 INSULATION

1X6 T&G HEMLOCK

1X4 BASE MOLDING

2X6 T&G FLOOR

18" CEDAR SHINGLES

½" PLY.

FLASHING BEDDED IN CAULKING

4X6 P.T.

2X4 ADDED FOR FLOOR SUPPORT

WALL SECTION

FIREPROOF TILE, SLATE OR CEMENT

8"X8" RED TILE FLUE

USED BRICK

3" CONCRETE BASE

Roofing

1. The roof over the main room is covered with 18″-long cedar shakes with a 7½″ exposure.

2. Since the roof of the potting shed has a low pitch, cover it with two layers of roll roofing before nailing on cedar shakes.

3. To provide more light for the potting shed, install 2′×2′ Plexiglas skylights between the rafters.

4. Use aluminum flashing around the chimney and the skylights and where the two roofs meet.

5. Build a 30″×30″ cupola out of scrap wood and leftover cedar shakes. Although this is purely decorative, it provides a perfect place to mount your favorite weathervane.

Windows and Doors

1. Salvaged windows can often be found and refurbished to suit your needs, or you can make your own (see page 15). Mount them in the window openings. Obviously, you should have the windows before beginning construction so you will know what size the openings should be.

2. You can also use salvaged doors, but David Hense's little house features an elegant homemade door with a window. The door is made from three layers of wood. The inside and outside layers are 1x4 rough-sawn hemlock nailed to a core of ¾″ exterior plywood. A small salvaged window can be set into the door, as shown, to let more light into the house.

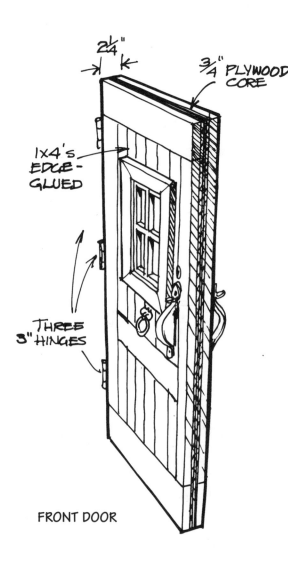

2¼″

¾″ PLYWOOD CORE

1x4's EDGE-GLUED

THREE 3″ HINGES

FRONT DOOR

CHAPTER 9

A Special Place

Time and space — time to be alone, space to move about — these may be the greatest scarcities of tomorrow.

Edwin Way Teale, *Autumn Across America*

Campfire Circle

Almost all primitive societies have had a special place where people can gather for meetings and ceremonies. It is generally a small area that has been cleared of underbrush and provided with some kind of seating. It could be on a mountain top, in the woods or facing the ocean. Although not essential, it is nice to have a focal point, such as a totem pole or wind sculpture — or simply a blazing campfire to roast marshmallows over. Today, this circular gathering spot could be used for a number of functions — a meeting place for a choral group, a poetry club, a meditation group, or a place for campers to cook out, meet, and discuss the events of the day. In Turkey, tree stumps are placed in a circle next to the sea, and apple tea is served after dinner.

The oval brick fireplace, open at both ends for ventilation, is a practical design for cooking, since the bricks can be lowered as the fire burns down, placing the grill closer to the embers.

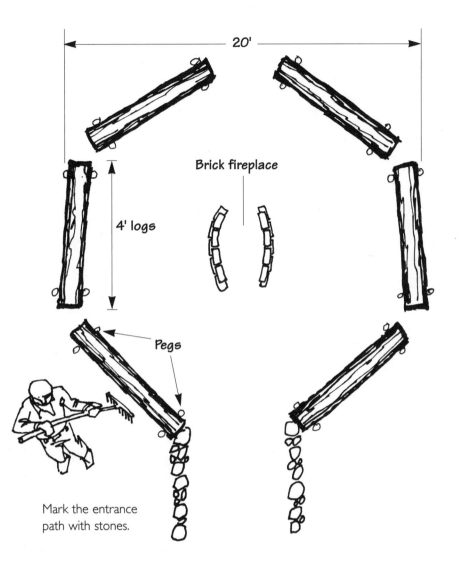

20'

Brick fireplace

4' logs

Pegs

Mark the entrance
path with stones.

Arranging the Circle

1. Clear a flat 20′ circular area of all underbrush. Level the area with a pick and shovel, and lay down a mulch (such as pine needles) to keep weeds out.

2. Cut six 12″-diameter logs, 4′ long, and place them around the circle.

3. Support the logs on flat rocks to prevent rot, and drive pegs in the ground to keep them from rolling.

PEGS

Wind Sculpture

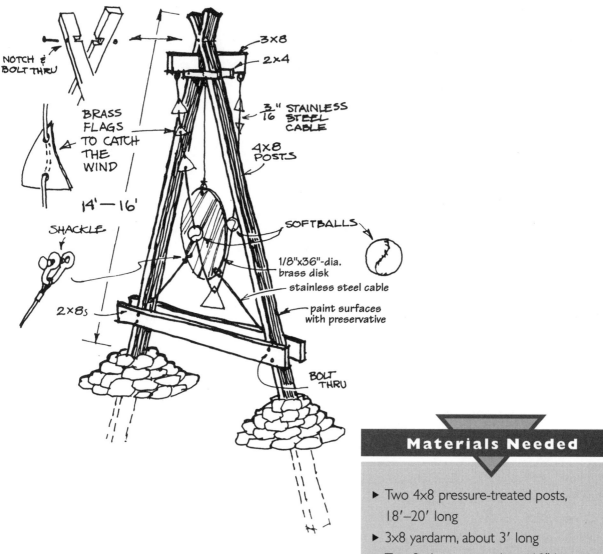

NOTCH &
BOLT THRU

BRASS
FLAGS
TO CATCH
THE
WIND

14' — 16'

SHACKLE

2×8s

3×8

2×4

3/16" STAINLESS
STEEL
CABLE

4×8
POSTS

SOFTBALLS

1/8"×36"-dia.
brass disk

stainless steel cable

paint surfaces
with preservative

BOLT
THRU

There are limitless ways to make a wind sculpture. The idea is to have the wind move something, whether it be a whirligig or a weather vane. In this design, the wind moves a softball, causing it to strike a large brass gong.

Wood pipes, glass chimes, bells, piano sounding boards, all can be made into interesting wind sculptures, depending on your musical taste.

Materials Needed

- ▶ Two 4×8 pressure-treated posts, 18'–20' long
- ▶ 3×8 yardarm, about 3' long
- ▶ Two 2×4 supports, about 18" long
- ▶ Two pieces of 2×8, 8'–10' long
- ▶ ½"×16" bolt
- ▶ ½"×8" bolt
- ▶ Four ½"×12" bolts
- ▶ Three shackles
- ▶ Five 3" eye screws
- ▶ Two softballs
- ▶ Disk and flags cut from ⅛" brass plate
- ▶ ⅛" stainless steel cable
- ▶ ³⁄₁₆" stainless steel cable

1. Clear a space for the wind sculpture in an open, windy spot.

2. Dig holes 3′–5′ deep for the posts.

3. Mark and notch the posts at the top, drill through the notches, and bolt them together.

4. Bolt two wooden braces to the posts a couple of feet above ground level.

5. Bolt the yardarm at the apex of the triangle inside the posts. Nail a 2×4 under it on each side for additional support.

6. Raise the posts with their bottoms in the holes. Make sure the structure is vertical, then fill the holes and brace the posts with stones. Use preservative on all wooden surfaces.

7. Drill three holes in the brass disk for shackles and suspend the disk between the posts using steel cable and eye screws.

8. Suspend the softballs and brass flags on another cable connected to the ends of the yardarm and looped under the disk.

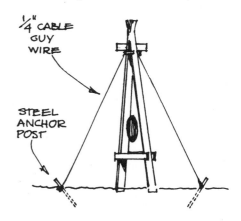

If the ground is too hard to bury the posts, use guy wires and anchor posts for support.

Your Special Place

By now you probably realize that we believe almost anyplace can be special. It doesn't matter where it is — on a mountain, in the woods, on the water, or in your own backyard — what makes it special is the meaning and the memories it has for you.

We hope that some of the designs in this book will strike your fancy and inspire you to build a rustic retreat of your own. If you do, we'd like to see it, whether it looks just like one of our designs or entirely different. Send us a photograph and, if you like, some information about your experience — what you wanted to do, how you went about it, and how it worked out. We would really enjoy hearing from you. Write to:

David and Jeanie Stiles
c/o Storey Communications, Inc.
Schoolhouse Road,
Pownal, VT 05261

Bibliography

Books

American Boys Handy Book, The. D.C. Beard. Charles E. Tuttle Co., Rutland, VT, 1966. Terrific ideas for kids to make and do.

Architectural Graphic Standards. Charles G. Ramsey & Harold R. Sleeper. John Wiley & Sons Publishing Co., Salt Lake City, UT, 1970. The Architect's Bible.

Build a Yurt. Len Charney. Collier Books, New York, NY, 1974. The best book you can find on the subject.

Building Small Barns, Sheds & Shelters. Monte Burch. Garden Way Publishing, Pownal, VT, 1983. A practical guide to building barns and acccessory buildings.

Building Thoreau's Cabin. Stephen Taylor. Pushcart Press, Wainscott, NY, 1992. A philosophical description of one man's experience in building a small cabin (not Thoreau's!).

Handmade Houses. Art Boericke & Barry Shapiro. Scrimshaw Press, San Francisco, CA, 1973. Color photos of many owner-built houses — beautiful!

How to Build a Low-Cost House of Stone. Lewis and Sharon Watson. Stonehouse Publications, Sweet Idaho, 1974. Details on stone house building.

How to Build and Furnish a Log Cabin. Ben Hunt. Collier Books, New York, NY, 1974. Building a log cabin using only hand tools.

How to Build Your Home in the Woods. Bradford Angier. Hart Publishing Company, New York, NY, 1952. Log cabin construction.

Indian Tipi, The. Its History, Construction & Use. Reginald & Gladys Laubin. Ballantine Books, New York, NY, 1957. The best book written on the subject.

Low-Cost Pole Building Construction. Ralph Wolfe, Garden Way Publishing, Pownal, VT, 1980. The best source for structures built on poles.

Native American Architecture. Peter Nabokov & Robert Eaton. Oxford University Press, New York, NY 1989. The best available information on Native American structures. Highly recommended, wonderful photographs.

Robin Hood Handbook, The. Bill Kaysing. Link Books, New York, NY, 1974. Tips on how to live in the wilderness.

Sheds — The Do-It Yourself Guide for Backyard Builders. David Stiles. Firefly Books, Ltd., Willowdale, Ontario, Canada, 1996. Everything you need to know about building a shed, including materials lists, step-by-step illustrated instructions, and photographs.

Shelter. Shelter Publications, Mountain Books, Santa Barbara, CA, 1973. An excellent book specializing in shelters of all kinds.

Shelters, Shacks & Shanties. D. C. Beard. Charles Scribner's Sons, New York, NY, 1972. The granddaddy of huts in America — an old book but worth re-reading.

A Shelter Sketchbook: Timeless Building Solutions. John S. Taylor. Chelsea Green, White River Junction, VT, 1997.

Stone Shelters. Edward Allen. The MIT Press, Cambridge, MA, 1981. A description of shelters hand-built out of stone indigenous to an area in southern Italy.

Thatchers & Thatching. Judy Nash, B. T. Batsford Ltd., London, England, 1991. For a more thorough description of thatching.

The Wilderness Cabin. Calvin Rutstrum. Collier Books, New York, NY, 1974. Information on more or less permanent structures built in the woods.

Tree Houses — You Can Actually Build. David & Jeanie Stiles. Houghton Mifflin Publishing, Boston, MA, 1998. The ultimate book on building your own tree house, including illustrations and photographs.

Woodcraft & Camping. Bernard S. Mason. Dover Publications, Inc., New York, NY, 1974. A very good book on Indian lore, camping, and shelters.

Woodstock Handmade Houses. Robert Haney & David Ballantine. Ballantine Books, New York, NY, 1974. Excellent color photographs of handmade houses.

Periodicals

Heartland USA, 174 Middlesex Turnpike, Burlington, MA 01803. Information and articles on everything that has to do with the outdoors, from structures to sports.

Cottage Life, 111 Queen St. East, Toronto, Ontario, Canada M5C 1S2. 416-360-6880. Cottage and projects oriented toward living on lakes.

Catalogs

Campmor, P. O. Box 700J, Saddle River, NJ 07458-0700. Camping equipment.

Defender Industries, Inc., 255 Main St., New Rochelle, NY 10801. Marine supplies.

L. L. Bean, Freeport, ME 04032. Camping equipment.

Silvo Hardware Co. 107–109 Walnut St., Philadelphia, PA 19106. Good complete catalog with prices.

Woodcraft. 313 Montvale Ave., Woburn, MA 01801. Hand tools for the very serious woodworker.

Harbor Freight Tools, 3491 Mission Oaks Blvd., Camarillo, CA 93011. 800-423-2567. Some of the best prices on hand and power tools.

Other Storey Titles You Will Enjoy

Small House Designs: Elegant, Architect-Designed Homes, 33 Award-Winning Plans, 1,250 Square Feet or Less, edited by Kenneth R. Tremblay, Jr. & Lawrence Von Bamford. This impressive collection of plans is useful for consumers and professionals alike. This book offers 34 cutting-edge designs produced by a worldwide array of architects, designers, and architecture students. 192 pages. Paperback, ISBN 0-88266-966-4; Hardcover, ISBN 0-88266-854-4.

Build Your Own Low-Cost Log Home, by Roger Hard. Recognized as one of the best books on this popular subject, *Build Your Own Low-Cost Log Home* features both line drawings and photographs. The author offers pages of options to help you create beautiful and affordable log house designs. 208 pages. Paperback. ISBN 0-88266-399-2.

Monte Burch's Pole Building Projects, by Monte Burch. This book covers every aspect of construction for more than 25 low-cost plans. Projects include garden structures, backyard barns, Victorian cabins, and sheds and shelters. 208 pages. Paperback. ISBN 0-88266-859-5.

Timber Frame Construction: All About Post-and-Beam Building, by Jack Sobon and Roger Schroeder. This book explains the basics of timber-frame construction in terms a beginner can understand: framing; designing for strength and beauty; using modern tools; and selecting the appropriate wood. 208 pages. Paperback. ISBN 0-88266-365-8.

How to Build Small Barns & Outbuildings, by Monte Burch. This book offers complete plans for 20 projects, including 70 photos and 150 line drawings. 288 pages. Paperback. ISBN 0-88266-774-2.

64 Yard & Garden Projects You Can Build Yourself, by Monte Burch. Award-winning author Monte Burch has created backyard building projects that even a beginner can tackle, from plant stands and cold frames to fences and greenhouses. Includes line drawings, photos, tables, lists, and maps. 192 pages. Paperback. ISBN 0-88266-846-3.

HomeMade: 101 Easy-to-Make Things for Your Garden, Home, or Farm, by Ken Braren and Roger Griffith. This book contains complete, easy-to-follow directions that will save you time and money. Projects include a lawn chair, compost bin, and movable shed. 176 pages. Paperback. ISBN 0-88266-103-5.

Play Equipment for Kids: Great Projects You Can Build, by Mike Lawrence. More than 30 easy-to-build projects for home, patio, and yard. Color plans and photos, plus exploded how-to drawings, show how to make attractive, durable swings, see-saws, climbing frames, playhouses, sandpits, and more. 96 pages. Paperback. ISBN 0-88266-916-8.

Be Your Own House Contractor, by Carl Heldmann. In this book, learn trade secrets on buying land, making estimates, getting loans, picking subcontractors, and buying materials and supplies. 144 pages. Paperback. ISBN 0-88266-266-X.

Be Your Own Home Renovation Contractor: Save 30% without Lifting a Hammer, by Carl Heldmann. This book explains how to find and appraise a restorable structure, obtain financing, and hire subcontractors. It includes sample contracts, bids, inspection reports, insurance forms and blueprints. 176 pages. Paperback. ISBN 1-58017-024-2.

These and other Storey books are available at your bookstore, farm store, garden center, or directly from Storey Books, Schoolhouse Road, Pownal, Vermont 05261, or by calling 1-800-441-5700. www.storey.com